THE SOCIAL DESIGNER'S PARADOX

WHY SOCIAL DESIGNERS MATTER AND STRUGGLE IN PUBLIC ORGANISATIONS

WILLEMIJN BROUWER

Colofon

Design inside and outside by: Willemijn Brouwer

Graphics by: Willemijn Brouwer

Copy edit by: Pieter van Knippenberg

Contact

Willemijn Brouwer, willemijn@williswijs.nl

www.thesocialdesignersparadox.com

BIS Publishers

Timorplein 46

1094 CC Amsterdam

The Netherlands

bis@bispublishers.com

www.bispublishers.com

ISBN 9789063698805

Every reasonable attempt has been made to identify owners of copyright. Any errors or omissions brought to the publisher's attention will be corrected in subsequent editions.

THE SOCIAL DESIGNER'S PARADOX

WHY SOCIAL DESIGNERS STRUGGLE AND MATTER IN PUBLIC ORGANISATIONS

WILLEMIJN BROUWER

BIS PUBLISHERS

To

my dad: the diverger who taught me to keep my head in the clouds,

my mom: the converger who taught me to keep my feet on the ground,

and myself: for actually putting my ideas on paper with my head, heart and hands. We should applaud our efforts!

Before you start, read this

Dear Reader,

Designers, armed with good intentions and a touch of naiveté, dive headfirst into the chaos of governments, only to encounter obstacles along the way. What exactly is the value of designers working on societal issues? Describing the work of a doctor or police officer is as simple as reciting the alphabet. However, when it comes to unravelling the enigma of a designer's purpose working in or with governments, we find ourselves lost in a labyrinth of abstract words.
Caught in the crossfire between theory and practice, I have witnessed firsthand the comedy and tragedy that unfold. As an Industrial Product Design Engineer with a passion for society, I am guilty of advocating for design in governments and facilitating workshops that failed to make the impact I want. In my role as an educator, I have seen the earnest enthusiasm of students clash with the harsh realities of the field and experienced how brilliant academics produce abstract works that fail to reach practitioners.
So, here we are, on a noble quest to bring clarity to the murky swamps of social design. Driven by the mission to place more designers in strategic positions within governments, I think this book should exist for designers trying to make a positive impact the public domain.
I don't claim to hold the ultimate truth, nor pretending that this book meets strict academic standards. Whenever

possible, I've supported my claims with literature from design, creativity studies, public administration, and management & organisation. Other parts of what you'll read are grounded in field research—particularly within the context of the Dutch national government.

Over the past years, I've had one-on-one conversations with dozens of civil servants (none of them formally trained as designers) about creativity, innovation, and the ever-popular concept of 'Design Thinking' in government. I've spoken face-to-face with about twenty civil servants who do have a background in design—most of whom were educated in faculties rooted in industrial product design engineering. Beyond that, I've gathered insights from ongoing conversations on LinkedIn and other professional network, and mentored a handful of graduating social design students working with government clients (more, if you count projects in the broader public sector), . I've designed a couple of serious games commissioned by governmental bodies and facilitated dozens of sessions on creativity and design, all with civil servants as participants. And I've had valuable conversations with researchers in the field of design and public administration, teach creativity theory and train others to facilitate creative processes in the public sector. For context: I studied Industrial Design Engineering myself—so yes, I too was educated as an industrial product designer; my lack of engineering talent made me choose the organising part of designing.

This is the foundation of what you're about to read.

Because yes, I do believe there is a place for designers in

government. And no, it's not in the basement with the broken printer or in a policy lab somewhere in a creative hub. Designers can help accelerate the transitions we so desperately need.

This book, a labour of love and a testament to Human Creation, is my humble attempt to put social designers in the spotlight and explain their ways of making sense of the world. I hope to offer insights, reflections, and perhaps even a chuckle or two along the way. And even though the world isn't short on opinions about design these days, I believe this book brings something worth adding to the conversation—it is the book I wish to give to my younger self.

Yours truly,

Willemijn Brouwer

Strategic Product Design Engineer
Lecturer in Creativity & Designing for Societal Missions
Creativity Facilitator & Trainer
Hobbyist Philosopher
Dutch World-Citizen
Mother, Wife, Sister, Daughter, Friend
Human Being (not Resource, thank you)

Contents

‘Not until we are lost do we begin to understand ourselves.’

Henry David Thoreau

Prologue

Imagine a designer wanting to use her design skills for the common good. Her name is Francis. She tells her friends and family she is a 'social designer'.

Her friend James studied Public Administration and Sociology. Francis always found him a bit of a 'know-it-all' and teases him that he will always be a risk-averse study nerd. He works in the Ministry of Housing and Spatial Planning and has been working there for over ten years. He started out as a policy executor and made his way up the career ladder. James is currently in a position in which he is responsible for multiple programs on social housing. Now and then, he is in a meeting with the Minister to share his advice on the matter.

James helped Francis prepare for her job interview for a position in the government as a policy innovation officer for elderly care. Before the interview, Francis just knew she was going to nail it! Now, she is not so sure anymore.

We listen in to the conversation between the recruiter, Roy, and Francis, entering somewhere in the middle:

> 'So, what are your strengths?' asks Roy.
> 'I'm good at integrating, orchestrating, visualising and reframing[1]', says Francis with confidence.
> 'Can you give me an example?' says Roy, he has no idea what Francis means with the words.

1 Van Arkel and Tromp (2024).

‘Well, here you can see how I can visualise complex information.’ Francis puts a print of one of her visualisations on the table.
‘Oh wow, that looks beautiful’, says Roy. At the same time, he thinks: ‘Why would we need this type of picture? It costs a lot of time; we can outsource this.’
He smiles kindly so Francis keeps talking:
‘I made this visual as a result of several co-creative sessions with different stakeholders. The question was to create a new vision for collaboration in care for diabetic children. I organised and designed the co-creative sessions; that is how I orchestrate. And I have integrated all viewpoints into a visual. Moreover, in the sessions, it turned out that all stakeholders had different perspectives. I was able to get all these perspectives to the surface without making people feel political about it.’
‘So, you are an expert in organisational change issues then?’ Roy asks, who honestly didn’t understand what she just said.
‘Well, expert in organisational change, I never thought of it that way, but perhaps yes’, answers Francis. ‘I’m good at reframing, so I guess that is the same.’
‘How is that the same? What is reframing?’ asks Roy, who has a political, quite negative association with the term ‘framing.’
‘Reframing is looking from a different perspective’, Francis continues. ‘Taking another angle towards the problem. So often, the problem we define is not the real

problem we need to solve; we have already chosen a frame. To solve a problem, we need to take a different frame', explains Francis.
'But you do not decide what problems to solve; that is for politicians or your manager to decide', Roy says.
'OK, yeah, but that is not what I mean', tries Francis.
'I'm sorry, perhaps I misunderstood, but can you explain what you mean?' Impatience is getting the best of Roy.
'Well,... it is different...' Francis gets stuck.
'OK... is it like Design Thinking?' Roy tries. He has heard his colleagues talk about this method. 'You empathise with the user, right, and do Design Sprints?'
'That could be part of it, yes. But that does not give the complete picture. Designing is more than doing Sprints and empathising with the user. I'm also good at dealing with different stakeholders.'
'Not with me', Roy silently thinks.

-

'Hey, how was that job interview you did a few weeks ago?' James asks Francis.
'Didn't get the job', Francis sighs.
'I'm sorry. Did you use the term Design Thinking again? I told you not to do that.'
'No, the recruiter mentioned Design Thinking at one point. But I couldn't explain myself. I feel so frustrated. I strut around with a fancy Master's degree in Design,

taking me years of blood, sweat, and tears to obtain. But then, there are these folks who breeze through a quick three-day Design Thinking course, and I can't articulate why my expertise is light-years ahead of their crash course. It feels downright embarrassing.'

'Oh, right.' James does not know what to say.

0. Introduction

0.1 The Francis-James Situation

Francis is one of many designers motivated by a passion for contributing to the common good. She believes her knowledge and skills can provide significant value to governments and public sector organisations. However, when she ventures beyond her expertise in industrial product design into the public sector, Francis often feels her contributions are lost in translation. Her approaches are frequently misunderstood by colleagues like her friend James.

James finds himself in a challenging position. He aspires to combat poverty but is also navigating the complexities of working in government during a time dominated by social media, artificial intelligence, and neoliberalism. This era highlights the impact of human behaviour on nature, features ongoing proxy wars worldwide, and sees the rise of right-wing politicians disrupting democracies. As a program manager in the civil service, James feels that change is being imposed upon him, and he is eager to improve how his programs are structured. Yet, he grapples with limited decision-making power and struggles to determine the best course of action. Alongside some colleagues, he feels they are merely spinning their wheels. While they all agree that change is necessary, their meetings yield no actionable plans—only the conclusion that 'we need more information'. Consequently, they continue to gather data but find themselves in the same predicament at each subsequent meeting.

Francis jokingly suggests that he should hire her for assistance, pointing out that designers excel at navigating situations with uncertain outcomes.

James struggles to respond. Lacking a design background, he fails to see the connection between his work on social housing and Francis's expertise as an industrial product designer. He silently thinks that Francis does not grasp the political and complex nature of his situation. He laughs awkwardly, but in truth, he is becoming increasingly frustrated, feeling that she seems to understand his work better than he does.

Blind Spot

Francis wants to use all her strengths in her work habits within the context of government. However, a government operates differently from a business, and a citizen is not merely a consumer—though they can be the same person. The outcomes in government are not products, and the working dynamics differ from those Francis is accustomed to in her design background.

Designers like Francis are trained to empathise with the end users of their creations, yet they often overlook the importance of empathising with their collaborators and themselves. Their expertise primarily stems from understanding the world they are designing for, rather than the context of government—or any other public organisation—in which they are designing. Francis does not recognise that she carries her own biases and assumptions into these new environments. Ironically, while she claims to excel at seeing multiple perspectives, she fails to acknowledge her own. Her implicit values and norms, shaped by her design, education and experience in a different context. These have shaped her professional identity and influenced her approach to work. Transitioning into the realm of governance as a designer is akin to trying to fit a square peg into a round hole (see figure 1).

Figure 1: The obvious metaphor of trying to fit a square into a circle.

Express Your Value

In her efforts to articulate her value, Francis often resorts to vague terms like 'Design Thinking' or describes her work as 'a process' or 'an approach.'

Imagine if a chef were to say, 'I take a cooking approach to change, or I use Chef's Thinking.' It would be hilarious. Industrial product designers have broadened their scope to include service design and, more recently, the design of virtually everything[2]. However, when the content—the product—no longer serves as the defining point for designers like Francis, what remains to describe their professional practice? They are left with ambiguous descriptions of 'an approach.'

Process or Practitioner?

When Francis says, 'Trust the process', she unintentionally diminishes her own profession. What she truly means is, 'Trust me. I know what I'm doing, even if the process appears chaotic to you.' But does she truly know what she is doing in the context of governance? Why would James trust her to help him move forward? What distinguishes these social designers

2 Stappers, Sleeswijk Visser, & van Boeijen (2023) identified 77 labels of 'design.' They distinguish five elements of design practice: values (design for), resources (design from), outcomes (design of), methods or actors (design by), and application domains (design in). The 77 labels emerged from the industrial product design practice and excludes design practices like architecture and mechanical design engineering.

from change agents, creative managers, workshop facilitators, or simply intelligent colleagues?

By not asserting ownership of their practice, designers risk reducing their profession to something that could be learned in a three-day workshop—a method that anyone could follow if they adhere to the steps.

Francis feels adrift. She struggles to understand her own role as a practitioner and may even question whether she has one. Some designers grapple with this as an existential dilemma.

Eager to contribute to the common good, Francis sees national government as a suitable platform for her efforts. While she can bring value, paradoxically, she struggles to communicate that value effectively.

0.2 Cliché Presumptions

In her efforts to explain herself, Francis confronts common misconceptions about design and designers. Her cousin, a Managing Partner at a large consultancy with a master's degree in business administration, often resorts to clichés when discussing design. To him, a designer is either a fashionable man speaking in incomprehensible terms or a vibrant elderly woman in a black turtleneck and trendy thick-framed glasses.

The image of a problem-solving designer dedicated to making a positive societal impact is far from his mind. Honestly, we can understand why.

To the general public, designers are often perceived as artists within the broader 'creative industry'. When those unfamiliar with the field talk about design, they tend to empathise aesthetics, associating designers with fashion, furniture, or sleek tech products.

This perception is not surprising; we frequently differentiate designer bags not by their functionality or ability to meet needs but by their appearance. Design is often experienced primarily as style—a visual signature that conveys brand identity. This applies not only to luxury items like Louis Vuitton bags but also to Apple devices and Danish chairs favoured by Northern European elites.

For many non-designers, the products designers create are viewed as utilitarian art—akin to a painter's canvas.

We might wish to dismiss this narrow view of designers as outdated, but social designers encounter these clichés daily, often being asked to make 'things pretty.' How can one begin to explain that it is entirely reasonable for designers to engage with societal challenges when faced with such a limited perspective? The nuanced role of designers like Francis is frequently overlooked—not only by her frustrating cousin at her uncle's birthday but also by professionals familiar with Design Thinking, who may misinterpret her value.

'You Do Design Thinking' Presumptions

In the 1980s, scholars in business management recognised the value of design principles in complex situations and thought, 'This is interesting. What can we learn from design?'

A management-centric version of design emerged as a new

body of knowledge, selecting certain elements to be used in business contexts. 'Design Thinking' created a parallel narrative that existed alongside design theory that educated designers. The rise in popularity of Design Thinking also contributed to the rise of social designers. Simultaneously, this version of design contributed to misunderstandings between designers like Francis and non-designers.

Francis does not recognise herself in these versions of 'Design Thinking'[3]. It oversimplifies her professional practice and leads to situations in which designers are asked to do specific tasks.

- 'You're a designer? Great, then you can facilitate that creative workshop.'
- 'You're a designer? Awesome, can you talk to some users for us?'
- 'You're a designer? Perfect, you do the layout and make the figures for our report.'

These tasks are *part* of their practice but do not *define* their practice. It is like asking a professional chef to cut the carrots, taste a dish, or boil the potatoes. Yes, it is part of the job but not a good representation of being a professional chef.

For Francis to sell herself into job positions in which she can make more of an impact, she needs to be able to respond to both her six-figure cousin and these professionals who have heard of Design Thinking but miss the essence. And to her friend James, who wants to understand her but simply doesn't.

For Francis to sell herself into job positions in which she can

---

3 Kimbell (2011), and Johansson-Sköldberg et al. (2013).

make more of an impact, she needs to be able to respond to both her six-figure cousin, as well as to these professionals who heard of Design Thinking but miss the essence. And to her friend James, who wants to understand her but simply doesn't.

0.3. Focus of the Book

'Social'

The term Social Design has been around for over seventy years but gained more traction in the past few decades[4]. In this book, the term Social refers to 'working for the common good'. The sociologists among us may not agree with this shortcut, and perhaps for some, the term has negative associations. I could have chosen a different term than Social Design for the title of my book. But 'Designers-that-use-their-practice-knowledge-skills-and-attitude-to-contribute-to-the-common-good' was simply too long.

Civil Service of Sovereign Governments

For the characteristics of the context, I focus on the civil service of state governments. In designing for the common good, the institution of the State Government is an important stakeholder. Societies have shaped their institutions, and institutions have shaped society. Institutions define how we organise our societies and function as the backbone of our

4 Tromp & Vial (2022).

societies. Rules, regulations, and the organisation of our institutions define 'the rules of the game'[5]. A government is the ultimate representation of a society. Yet, a government does not consist of one type of organisation. Since there are more positions to be filled in civil service than there are in politics, I focus on the public administration[6] of a State government. Other public organisations will showcase some similarities with civil service. Thus, for those social designers who do not (want to) work directly in or for public administration, the civil service serves as a showcase for other public organisations as well.

Person

I choose a person's perspective on social design, which is why the title of the book is The Social Designer's Paradox, and not the Social Design Paradox.

Design as a noun and designing as a verb describe a result or process as something that is there or happens. It creates a distance between what people do, say, and make designing happen. Objectifying the blood, sweat, and tears people put into their work as designers seems undesignerly to me[7].

5 Moerman & Brouwer (2005, p. 16).

6 Public administration refers to the systems, principles, and processes guiding government operations, while the civil service comprises the professionals who carry them out in practice. I will use both terms.

7 See chapter 5 for why it seems undesignerly.

Not any Designer

When we talk about design in general, we not only overlook the designers but also what is actually being designed. Is it a garment, a democratic system, an industrial product, or a poster? We tend to group all designers together, ignoring the specific nature of their work. Design scholars do the same. The existing body of knowledge on design assumes that designing is a universal activity—independent of what is being designed (chapter 1). However, knowledge, skills, attitudes, and expertise are shaped by the specific practice of each design discipline. An architect works differently from a mechanical engineer, a graphic designer, or an industrial product designer. As a result, each develops distinct competencies and ways of thinking. Also, norms and values differ per design practice. The type of Social Designer I refer to is trained in the tradition of Industrial Product Design. This field originally focused on people as consumers and on creating value through mass-producible products (chapter 5). Designers from this background have since expanded their practice beyond industrial products into other areas. Whenever I use the word 'designer', I mean these types of designers. Francis is one of them.

Reflexive

Unlike the trendy 'How to be a designer in 10 steps' type of books, this book focuses on what lies beneath the steps. That is not a quick fix, but more of a reflexive nature. Designers use reflection in their work to decide upon the next steps. The Social Designer's Paradox is a moment to stop running and

Social Designers are professional practitioners, educated in the legacy of Industrial Product Design, who apply their knowledge, skills, and mindsets to create a positive impact for the common good, by working in/for a national government.

think.

To quote the author of Jurassic Park[8]: 'Without history, you are a leaf that doesn't know it's part of a tree.'

In the Social Designer's Paradox, I use two legacies from a design perspective: the one from design science, under the premise that design is a universal trait, and the legacy of Industrial Product Design as a specific design discipline. I use traditions from public administration to describe the general legacies that influence the way of working in governments.

In the words of ABBA, Francis and James need a little: 'Knowing me, knowing you'.

> 'I'm sorry. Hi, can I interrupt here just one second?'
>
> *'Oh, hi Francis. Yes, go ahead.'*
>
> 'They don't know that James and I are also in this book, do they?'
>
> *'You mean our readers? Well, they know you are the personification of the Social Designer I'm writing this book for. But they don't know you and James have a voice. Now they know :) Is that why you interrupted?'*

---

8 Michael Chrichton.

'No, I'm sorry, I only wanted to check...because you said that you will refer to legacies and use words like 'history'...well, you're not going to be boring, are you? I mean, if I were into history, I would have chosen a different profession.'

'I see your point. Realise that legacies explain why you make different assumptions than James, why you act differently, think differently, and why your norms and values are different. Your mental models and normal ways of doing were formed in these legacies.

Imagine you are a product. But you don't understand the function of yourself as a product. Then you are put in a context where people have never seen you before; they only know you from a distance and in completely different surrounding. They have no idea what they can use you for, and since you can't explain your function yourself, you end up in the drawer or trash can. Therefore, it is handy to understand the product (yourself) and the context a bit better, don't you agree?'

'Yes, I get that... But just please don't be boring, okay?'

'I don't plan to. I'm sure our readers also prefer a book that is not boring. If you need to interrupt me along the way, feel free to do so. I will edit unconstructive interruptions after we are done anyway. So, you can tell me when I'm boring you. Same goes for you, James. James? James?!'

'Hi, yes, I'm here. Sorry, I had an urgent email I needed to respond to. I'm putting my phone away, right... now.'

'Ha! You always have an urgent email', Francis responds.
'You're in, James?'
'Yes. Francis is right, my apologies again. I'm in, focused.'
'Great! And to our readers, I hope you enjoy the conversations Francis and James bring. I believe their reflections will add an extra layer to our story. I will answer some of your questions through them.'
'Can you also keep the drawings? I like the way you drew me. I seem perky even though I'm a stick figure. But I don't often wear a tie, okay?'
'Yes, James, I'll add the drawing to the text and I will leave the tie out next time.'
'Thanks.'
'You're welcome.'

0.4 Legacies in a Nutshell

Traditions in Public Administration[9]

The evolution of norms, values, and ways of working in Western government can be traced through four distinct periods (see figure 2), with each one adding a new layer of complexity (and a few headaches).
After World War I, bureaucracy reigned supreme (constitutional tradition). The civil service was all about

9 Braams (2021), and Stout (2017).

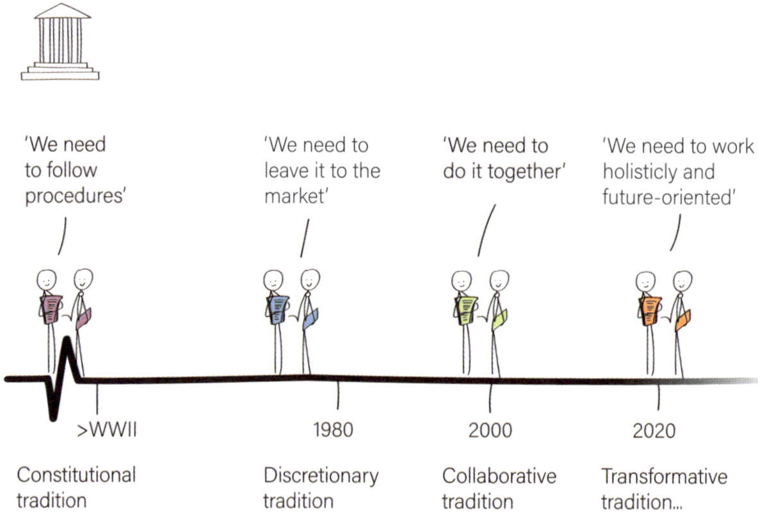

Figure 2: Overview of four traditions in public administration.

structure, rules, and treating everyone equally: fairness through form-filling.

Then came the 1980s, when governments took a sharp turn towards the private sector (discretionary tradition). Inspired by neoliberal ideas, they tried to behave more like businesses, embracing efficiency, performance metrics, and a newfound love of management jargon.

In the 2000s, digital technology promptly stirred the pot. Things became more complex, and governments found themselves needing to collaborate with private companies, non-profits, and basically all sorts of organisations to help move forward in the web of the public domain (collaborative tradition).

Now, we find ourselves in a period where change is constant, fast, and often confusing. Governments are challenged to govern in real-time, juggling innovation, unpredictability, and a never-ending stream of 'new normals', leading us to a new tradition in the making: the transformative tradition.

Legacies from Design Science[10]

In the same year that Americans first landed on the moon, design emerged as a science. The breakthrough came with the publication of 'The Sciences of the Artificial' by Herbert Simon. But a decade before, design was a topic of scholarly interest. The main idea was that designing was a systemic process of optimising and planning. If you examine design methods from that period, you will encounter numerous diagrams of blocks and arrows.

Design scholars identified the 1973 article by Rittel & Webber[11] on Wicked Problems as the saviours of the discipline. The design scholars at that time argued that the first wave of design methods was over, and that we had now entered the second wave. This allowed for the abandonment of previous ideas while still keeping the design discipline alive.

In the 1980s, books on design methods and journals on design emerged, consolidating design as a scientific discipline. In the same period, a third wave of design research emerged from the popularity of cognitive psychology: if we understand how

10 Cross (2007), and Lloyd (2017), see figure 3 for an overview of the legacies in Design Science.

11 Rittel & Webber (1973), also see chapter 4.

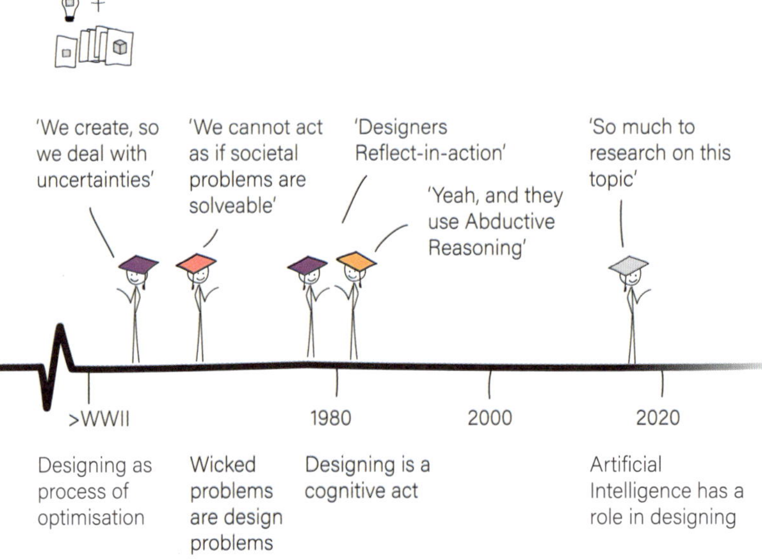

Figure 3: Overview of the three (to four) focus areas in the science of design.

designers think, we can design better.
When artificial intelligence became accessible to a larger audience around 2020, the focus shifted from human cognition to the role of AI in designing and how designers can use AI.

Legacies from Industrial Product Design

Industrial product design emerged post-WWII as mass production and economic recovery fuelled demand for desirable products. As markets saturated in the decades after WWII, designers shifted from problem-solving to problem-finding, uncovering latent consumer needs. The concept of Wicked Problems in design theory was especially adopted by industrial product designers[12] as early as the beginning of the 1990s[13]. Around the turn of the millennium, industrial product design expanded to include service design, using digital elements. By the 2020s, industrial product designers expanded their scope to many different fields. See figure 4 for an overview of the legacies from industrial product design.

The worlds of governing and designing have converged in the past decades. Business administration gained interest in the way designers work as early as the 1980s. When governments adopted a business mindset, design consultancies began offering service design as a more general service. This increased governments' interest in design, creating space for designers like Francis, but at the same time left Francis in a state of confusion.

0.5 Structure in Four Parts

The Social Designer's Paradox is divided into four parts, each inspired by a different tradition in public administration. The structure loosely follows a chronological timeline, helping you to see how things have evolved and where they might go next. The purple section explores the foundations of both governing

12 Cross (2007).

13 Buchanon (1992).

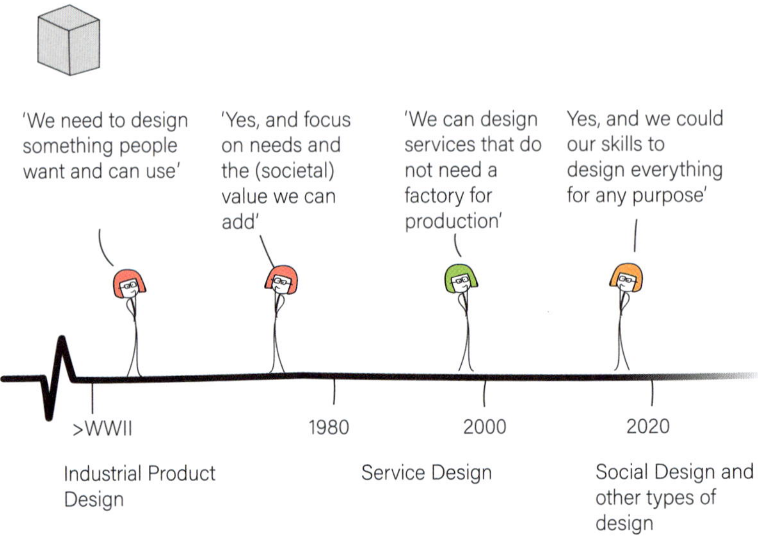

Figure 4: Overview of legacies from industrial product design.

and designing, taking us up to the 1980s. This is where the groundwork was laid.

The blue section delves into the rise of neoliberalism and how it shaped a new way of thinking in public administration. It also examines the emergence of wicked problems and discusses industrial product design as a distinct design discipline, roughly from 1980 to 2000.

The green section looks at the early 2000s to 2020, when collaborative approaches began to take hold. Here, public administration and service design started to merge, designers trained in the industrial mindset began to shift their role.

The orange section focuses on the present, or rather the ever-changing Dynamic Quo. A new tradition in public administration is forming and social designers are finding

new ways to contribute. This part also considers what social designers do differently.
Figure 5 provides a visual overview of these four traditions, with the same colours representing their respective parts. Each part will end with a summary of 'inherited baggage', values, beliefs and norms that form the way Francis and James work. To keep the overview, each part ends with a table[14] containing the leading principles in the world of James and in the world of Francis, what gets designed, by and for whom, how it's made real, and the context in which it all happens. In the final part of the book, 'Say It With a Song', I draw conclusions for Francis and James about how they can help each other to flourish.

Paradoxes

In the course of this story of legacies paradoxes arise. At first glance, the way this story is structured may seem dualistic—perhaps even oppositional. Governing and designing appear to stand on opposite sides. One belongs to the realm of systems and institutions; the other, to the actions of individuals. Public administration operates at the level of society, while design is rooted in personal agency. In that sense, one is context, the other is action.
This might suggest contradiction, even incompatibility. But is it really a contradiction when we're comparing two fundamentally different things? It's like comparing apples to

14 See pages 38-39 for an empty version of the overview table.

Figure 5: Overview of three legacies combined.

pears—different in nature, yet both part of the same basket. And that's where it gets interesting.

If we shift our perspective and approach the comparison with creativity, what once seemed irreconcilable can, in fact, inform and enrich one another. The paradox lies not in the clash between governing and designing, but in the tension—and potential—between structure and creativity, between collective systems and individual initiative.

The Social Designer's Paradox is not one neat, singular contradiction. It's multi-layered, full of nuance, and often a little messy—which is exactly what makes it so engaging. It invites us to think beyond binaries and explore how seemingly incompatible ideas might coexist, challenge each other, and even lead to new forms of practice.

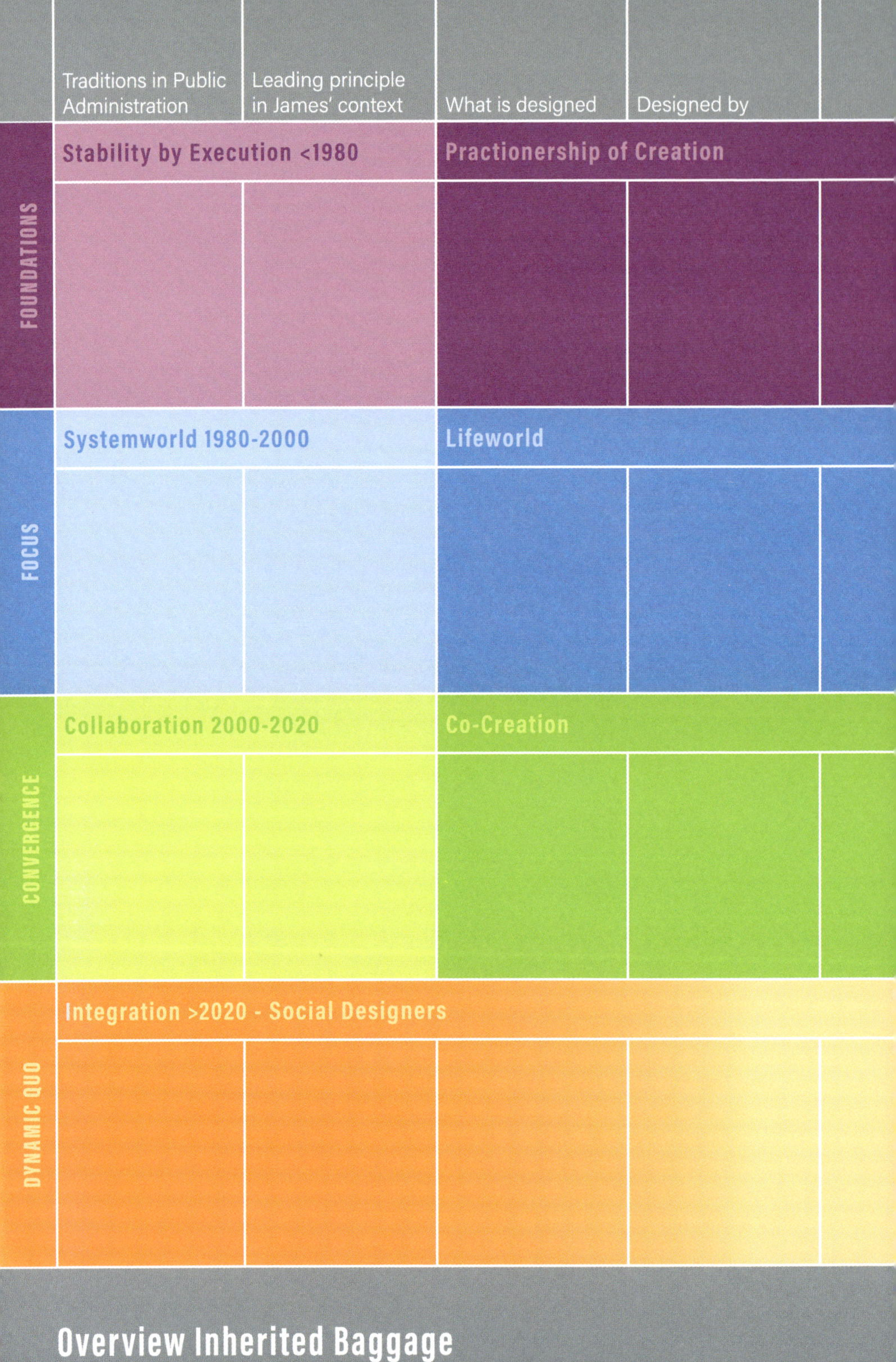
Traditions in Public Administration
Leading principle in James' context
What is designed
Designed by
FOUNDATIONS
Stability by Execution <1980
Practionership of Creation
FOCUS
Systemworld 1980-2000
Lifeworld
CONVERGENCE
Collaboration 2000-2020
Co-Creation
DYNAMIC QUO
Integration >2020 - Social Designers
Overview Inherited Baggage

	Leading principle in Francis' practice	Designed in the Context of (viability)	Designed for (desirability)	Design realised by (feasibility)

Foundations

<1980

Francis is a designer. James works in government. Their worlds are built on different foundations. Design is about creating what does not yet exist, while governing is about preserving stability. Francis thinks by doing. In her practice, thought and action go hand in hand. But James works in a system that separates the two. Plans are made at the top and carried out below—a legacy of factory floors and production lines.
The work of Francis and James differs not only in purpose, but also in the very foundations of how that work is organised.

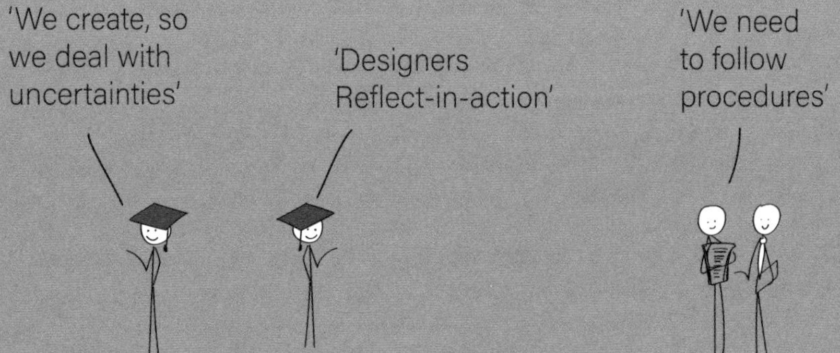

'We create, so we deal with uncertainties'

'Designers Reflect-in-action'

'We need to follow procedures'

1. Practitionership of Creation

1.1 What is Designing?

Stickers

In the Netherlands, we have our own Route 66. The A12 highway stretches from east to west, adorned with lanterns that sport colourful stickers (see figure 6). These stickers are striped in four colours from top to bottom: purple, red, dark green, and light green. Each colour symbolises something you pass on the journey: industry, houses, forests, and grasslands. We even call it 'The Rainbow Route'.

I laugh out loud, picturing civil servants in a 1980s meeting room brainstorming the name of this highway, debating the colour scheme of the stickers, and passionately discussing the CMYK values. These stickers were meticulously planned. We can question the relevance of these stickers, but the fact is:

Figure 6: Lanterns along the Rainbow Route (A12 highway) in the Netherlands. Photo by Mariëlle van Wijk.

they were 'designed.'

'Design' comes in a verb and a noun. I'll focus on the verb because we want to understand what designers are *doing*. Everything deliberately planned and created by humans falls under the umbrella of 'being designed' except other humans, for now at least. The streets we walk on, the pots we cook in, the phones we use as cameras: all these things were designed. But also democratic structures, organisational hierarchies, laws, and hospitals are results of human design actions.

What's in a Word?

In etymology, the art of tracing a word's journey through time, we find hidden narratives that shed light on the evolution of human thought. In other words, it is like digging into the family tree of words to uncover their roots and how they've grown over time. What can we say about the word 'designing' from an etymological perspective? Designing comes from the Latin 'de' and 'signare'. 'De' means to come into existence, to sprout. 'Signare' we know as a verb meaning 'to sign' or 'to mark'. So, picture planting a seed of an idea and marking it as your own, ready to blossom into something grand. In the Renaissance, we stumble upon 'disegnare', meaning both 'to plan, contrive' and 'to draw or paint'.

Defining Designing as Creating an Idea+Plan

Bruce Archer was among the first influential design researchers[15]. Archer defined design as a verb, stating that it involves *'conceiving an idea for and preparing a description of a proposed system, artifact, or aggregation of artifacts.'*[16] Designing encompasses two main elements: conceiving the idea and devising a plan to transform that idea into reality, in any form. The outcome can be a system, artifact, or an aggregation of artifacts. Therefore, technological knowledge and creative interventions together form the input to generate ideas and plans for results in various forms. Figure 7 showcases how this looks in a picture. The term technological knowledge showcases the design engineering perspective on designing. But technological knowledge may also refer to the knowledge and skills of the application field, like knowledge of mixing paint colours in the application field of painting.

---

15 Archer was not the only one; for example, see also Christopher Alexander and John Chris Jones, both pioneers in the science of design.

16 Archer (1968), page 9.

Bruce Archer

Bruce Archer earned a PhD in Industrial Design (Engineering) from the Royal College of Art. The inclusion of 'engineering' in parentheses may indicate why he pursued this degree at an Art College, as it might seem an unconventional choice. However, Archer asserted as early as the 1950s that industrial designers should draw on both art and science, striking a balance between creative invention and solid technological knowledge.

His groundbreaking thesis synthesised his previous fifteen years of published work. In this thesis, he aimed to develop an algorithmic framework for designing, driven by his relentless pursuit to comprehend the essence of designing.

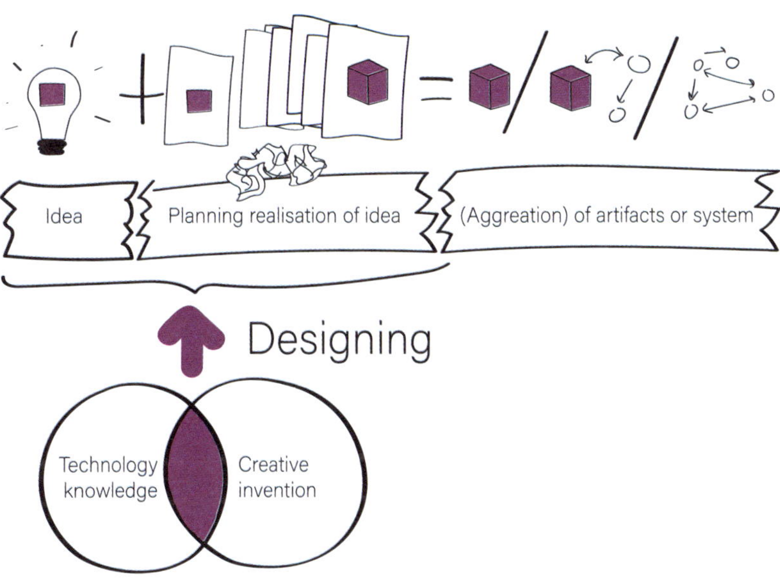

Figure 7: Designing interpreted from Archer (1968).

Designing is a Deliberate Creative Activity

Following this line of thinking, action painters like Jackson Pollock, who didn't plan for his paintings but went with the flow in the moment, do not qualify as designers. However, Picasso made many sketches before he painted La Guernica, which qualifies him as a designer.
The Homo sapiens who thought in advance about how to sharpen their rocks to create better axes were designers. The Homo sapiens who accidentally cut off a sharp piece and realised they could use it as an axe were not designers; they were simply paying attention. There is a form of deliberateness in design that is a special form of creative human activity. Paintings, urban areas, policies, recipes, industrial products, machines, poems, and more. They all stem from ideas and deliberate creations of the human mind; hence, they are all designed.

1.2 The Science of Design

The first Conference on Design Methods, held in London, UK, in 1962, aimed to identify commonalities in design practices across different application fields[17]. In the same year that Americans first landed on the moon, design also landed as a science. The landmark came with the publication of 'The Sciences of the Artificial' by Herbert Simon.

---

17 Conference on Design Methods (1963).

Herbert Simon was the type of genius who makes me question if he ever slept. A Nobel Prize laureate in economics, he also succeeded in cognitive psychology and computer science.
In 'The Sciences of the Artificial', Simon argues that while natural sciences like physics and biology seek to understand the natural world, and humanities seek to understand, well, humans, the science of the artificial is dedicated to comprehending what humans create – our products, systems, and even cities. Simon viewed design as a process of planning and problem-solving. Designing these artificial systems, he contends, is a science in its own right, necessitating specific methodologies and approaches.
Where natural sciences and humanities study the world as it is, students in these academic fields learn to do just that: study the world as it is and try to explain the world as it is. But designing is about creating a (new) world.

> Designing is about **changing** what is, while humanities and natural sciences are about **describing** what is.

The Unknown Objective

When designing, we create something that did not exist before. We can predict how materials will behave and calculate the exact length a beam needs to hold a specific weight. In some cases, determining the strength of a beam becomes challenging because we cannot accurately calculate how it will interact with the other design components. If we use materials in specific

FOUNDATIONS

Conference on Design Methods

The very title of the conference speaks to this goal. Contributors to the conference spanned various fields of engineering, as well as practitioners from diverse backgrounds (see figure 8). Two contributors were affiliated with an Art Academy, while two had a background in psychology. Four contributors represented companies, and one was an independent artist. Additionally, there were two painters, one planning officer, and one industrial design lecturer among the contributors. One notable lack of diversity among the contributors is the fact that they were all men, which, although unfortunate, is not surprising given the time period of the 1960s. Another noteworthy aspect is that all contributors were native English speakers. This linguistic homogeneity carries significance, as language encapsulates values. I will delve further into this topic in part three.

This 1962 conference is significant in design research as the inception of design as a scientific research discipline.

ways or assemble parts in specific orders, unexpected results occur. New arrangements of parts may lead to interactions full of surprises. This is why it is difficult to know all the objectives of our design result upfront, nor is the list of criteria for a solution clear from the beginning.

In Archer's words[18]: *'The complete set of objectives is only rarely definable at the beginning of the project. Most of them emerge by mutual consent as the project progresses.'*

---

18 Archer (1968), page 15.

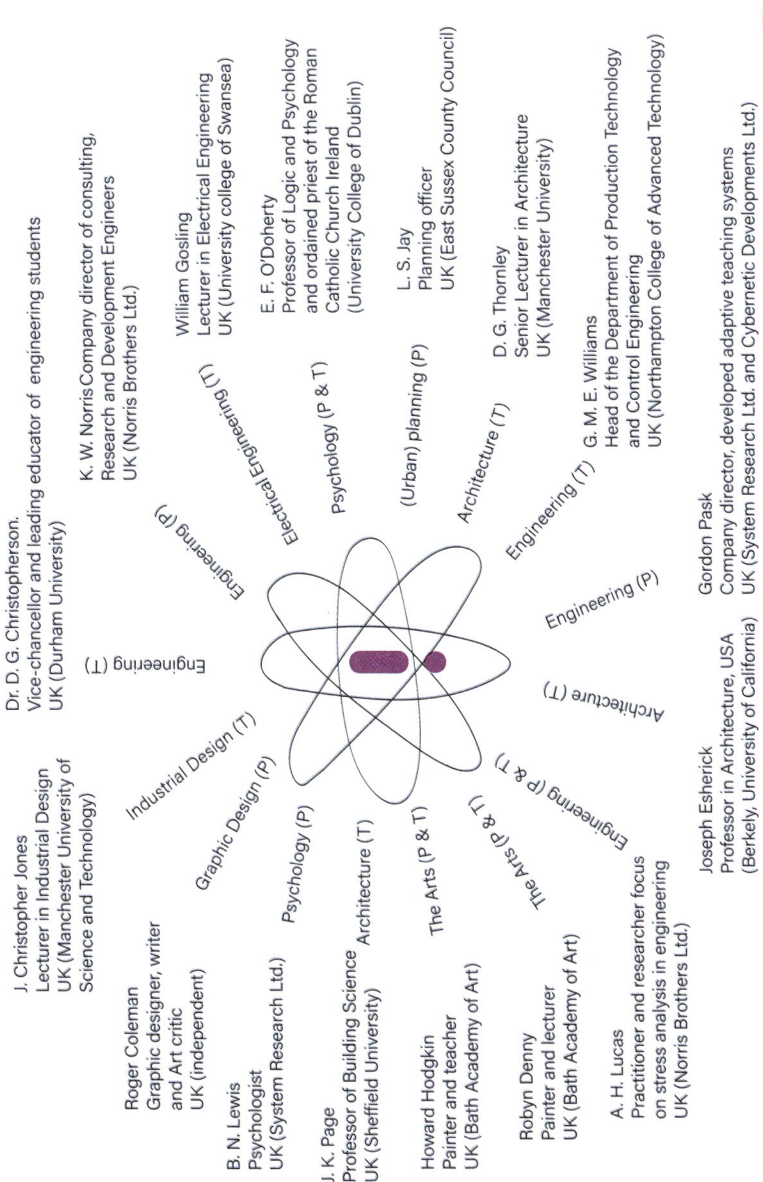

Figure 8: Overview contributors Conference on Design Methods 1962, P= perspective from practicc, T=perspective from theory.

Unknown Interaction Between Components

When designers create an artifact or system, they must consider the relationships between its various components in the artifact or various parts in a system. The components are interdependent, meaning that changes in one component can affect changes in other components. This is encapsulated in the idea that 'if I pull here, it moves over there.'
For example, while I want the artifact that I am designing to be lightweight, I also need it to be strong. To achieve strength, I might need to use a thicker beam, which requires more material and ultimately makes the product heavier. Solving one problem often creates another elsewhere in the design. I need to take interdependencies into account and try different ways of achieving strength, so I can also adhere to the lightweight criteria. Designing involves not just the individual elements but also how these elements relate to one another when assembled.

1.3 The Universality Presumption

Design researchers assume that designing transcends the specific application field of the design. This means that designing a building has commonalities with designing a product, designing a story, and designing an urban area. There is universality in designing[19]. Design, as a scientific discipline,

19 Buchanon (1992).

would not exist without this presumption.
It serves as the bedrock for the entire body of knowledge!

Satisfycing[20]

Simon introduced the term 'Satisfycing' to describe the effort to balance different criteria to reach a satisfactory outcome.
If I can adjust the design so that it scores satisfactory in strength and good in weight, this balance would be considered satisfactory. Not perfect, but satisfying. Simon's 'Satisfycing' refers to this process of achieving an acceptable balance between seemingly competing factors (see figure 9).

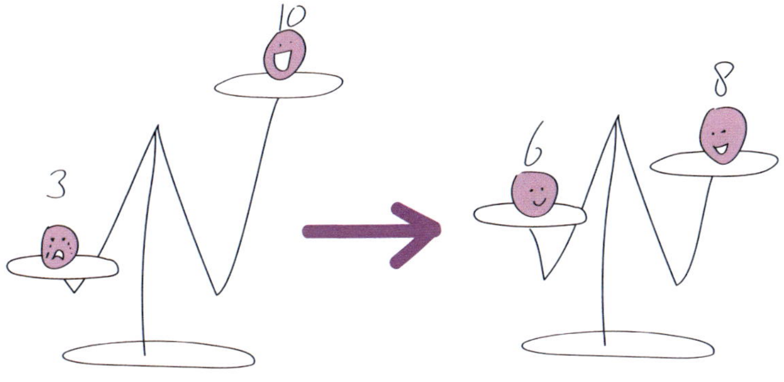

Figure 9: Satisfycing is like creating a new balance on the scale.

'So, if an idea and a plan define designing, why then is everybody a designer?' exclaims James. 'Let's go to the beach (idea) and let's take the bus instead of the car (the plan). I just designed the afternoon activity with my

20 Simon (1969).

friends.'

'If we were to ask Archer what designers design, his answer would be: 'anything'. So when you are designing a plan to go to the beach, you could say you are a designer. How do you feel about that, Francis?'

'Hm, I do see James as a designer, but not because he can come up with a plan to go to the beach. I see him as a designer because he makes public policies. I think a policy is an idea and a plan to execute the idea in reality; a policy is a design. So policy-making processes are design processes, and policy-makers are designers. The plan to go to the beach seems too easy, too trivial to be labeled as designing.'

'I actually agree', says James. 'It was kind of a joke. Designing seems more difficult than the example I gave. But I also don't think I'm a designer.'

'Thus, you two agree that designing needs some sort of expertise on what you are doing, because designing a plan to go to the beach is actually not designing because it is too simple. Anyone can do it?'

'Yes', says James.

'Perhaps a certain level of skill or knowledge is needed for me to call it designing', Francis thinks out loud.

'Okay. And you two disagree with the idea of James being a designer. Francis thinks policy-making is designing; James doesn't see that as designing. Correct?'

'Yes!' they say simultaneously.

'James, if designing needs expertise and comes with an idea and plan to create something, why don't you see policy-making as designing?'
'Because the 'something', as you call it, that I create is a text for a plan to regulate housing in a specific way or something like that. That is not something real.'
'You mean something tangible?'
'Yes, I work as a civil servant; it doesn't feel like I'm designing policies like a 'designer'.'
'Why do you use quotations when you say 'designer'?' Francis asks.
'Well, you know, designers are...'
'...like artists?' Francis finishes his sentence.
'Well, yeah', James realises his own perception of designers is exactly what we have been discussing earlier: the designer as artist, not as a human creator of ideas and plans.

Claiming that design is a universal act of human creation is quite a bold statement. On an abstract level, there may be truth to it. Designing a house or designing a housing policy could both be described as forming an idea and planning its realisation. But in practice, that definition doesn't get us very far. It overlooks the role of the design discipline itself. It suggests that what we design has no bearing on how we design, which is a flawed assumption.
In a tentative study, Jiang & Gero observed a design team composed solely of industrial product design students. When

FOUNDATIONS

faced with an open-ended design challenge, they spent about half of their time exploring and understanding the problem[21]. In contrast, mixed teams and teams of mechanical engineering students devoted almost all their time to solving the problem, focusing on the solution rather than the problem itself.
Why is this? Because what we design shapes how we design. So even if we talk about design as a universal concept, the actual process—how we think, make decisions, and move forward—is shaped by the nature of the thing being designed.
Creativity research generally agrees that there is a relationship between a person's expertise in a specific field and the level of creative output they can achieve[22]. In other words, how someone creates is closely tied to what they create. A great painter, for instance, may be highly creative in painting but not necessarily in music or even in drawing. Since designing is an act of human creation, the nature of what is being created matters.

What you design defines **how** you design.

'Francis, you were educated in the tradition of industrial product design. Would you say that this design discipline influences how you design?'
'I don't know. I only know this is my design discipline',

21 Jiang & Gero (2014).

22 Baer (2015).

says Francis.
'But you did design a vision for treating kids who are diabetic. I heard you say that in your job interview[23]. That is not an industrial product.'
'Oh yeah, right. I think I applied how I design a product to designing this vision', reflects Francis.
'On one hand, we can conclude that universality in designing does not do justice to the complexity of practice; on the other hand, you try to force-fit your way of working to create something different than a product. In a way, you then expect universality. If you look at it from this perspective, it is kind of weird why you think you can design a policy for elderly care when you are educated to design products.'
'Yes, I see your point. Perhaps that is what the recruiter was thinking as well. But you can see 'a vision for diabetic care' as a product. The same sort of processes to create this vision can be applied. I've done it; it works. Besides, industrial product design has developed over the years; I was not only educated to design products.'
'Of course, that part is for later[24]. And that process you mention, that can be applied, what then is that process?'
'Well, you know, the design process.'
'Which is...'
'Is that a trick question? I would say that the design

23 See prologue.

24 Part green: convergence, and part orange: integration

process is taking the human-centered perspective, integrating different stakeholders into one solution, empathising with your user, co-creating, and first diving into the problem before you try to solve it.'
'It was kind of a trick question; you're right. In your job interview, you said the same with different abstract words. That didn't get you the job.'

The universality often assumed in design research may hold at a cognitive or abstract level. But in practice, the values, skills, attitudes, and methods shaped by specific design disciplines influence the beliefs and working habits of different types of designers.
Designers are educated in a specific design discipline that revolves around creating something. Whether it's a product, a poster, a garment, or even a building, their work is organised around this 'something' they are shaping. Designers are practitioners; they have 'a practice.' As in any practice, thinking and doing are deeply intertwined. The head and hands are engaged in constant dialogue, and any passionate designer would agree that the heart plays a role too. In this way, design is a discipline where thought and action are not separate but integrated.

1.4 Practitionership

Practitioners have developed expertise through action and reflecting on that action. Whether in medicine, law, design, or sports, they operate within a specific practice, shaped by real-world contexts, experience, and continuous learning. Practitionership refers to the depth of ownership a practitioner has over their practice; the ability to not only perform tasks competently but to act with intuition, judgment, and a kind of embodied understanding that goes beyond textbook knowledge.

Reflection-in-Action[25]

The philosopher, educator, and architect Donald Schön gave this phenomenon a name: reflection-in-action. In his influential book, The Reflective Practitioner, Schön explored how professionals (from architects to psychotherapists) think in the midst of doing. Instead of pausing to analyse from a distance, they adjust, experiment, and respond in real time. Their thinking is embedded in action, not separate from it.
This is where practitionership comes in. It's not just applying knowledge like a recipe; it's the integration of thinking, doing, and being. Head, hands, and heart are woven into the moment of practice. It's where intuition meets experience, and learning happens inside the doing, not after the fact.
Practitioners (thus also designers) move in circles rather than

25 Schön (1987; original 1983), and Visser (2010).

straight lines. Their process loops back on itself: try something, see what happens, adjust, repeat.
Schön calls the actions that practitioners take 'moves'. These are not random steps, but purposeful actions shaped by experience. The more practiced someone is, the more they rely on this embodied knowing.

Mastery

We see this mastery clearly in fields like medicine or law, where seasoned professionals navigate complex, high-stakes situations with apparent ease. But we also recognise it in professional athletes—think of footballers like Johan Cruijff, Diego Maradona, or Zinédine Zidane. These players had a 'feel for the game'—a non-verbal, almost instinctive grasp of what was happening on the field and what needed to happen next. This kind of knowing is hard to articulate, yet unmistakable in action.

The iterative nature isn't a flaw; it is the essence of their creative practice. Every move teaches something, and each adjustment becomes part of learning. Practitionership thrives in this back-and-forth rhythm.
Schön shows that seasoned practitioners constantly adjust their actions based on subtle feedback, often without being able to explain exactly why. This is the realm of 'knowing that' rather than 'knowing how'. It's the difference between having a sense of what to do and following a manual.
Take doctors, for instance. You wouldn't say a good doctor

'follows a process' like assembling IKEA furniture. Sure, they may consult a checklist, but their diagnosis depends on practitionership: a trained intuition, honed by experience. Meanwhile, the rest of us are diagnosing ourselves with apps and a vague sense of dread. We've got the 'knowing how' (thanks, internet), but not the 'knowing that' that comes with real practitionership.

Expert practitioners[x] don't just follow a **process**—they have a **practice**.

[x]Fig 10: Example practitioners: a chef, judge, doctor, architect, professional football player, nurse, and a teacher.

Nothing New

Schön draws on philosophers from the past and claims he does not really say anything new. Reflection-in-action is like a learning cycle, and in his arguments, he stands on the shoulders of pragmatists like Peirce, Dewey, and Habermas. Schön also refers to Christopher Alexander, an early design scholar[26]:

---

26 Schön (1992), page 7.

FOUNDATIONS

'The remarkable ability of humans to recognise more in the consequences of their moves than they have expected or described ahead of time.'

People are able to imagine an outcome and compare the real outcome to what they imagined.

Peirce, Habermas, and Dewey in a Paragraph

Charles Sanders Peirce, an American philosopher and scientist, is known as the father of pragmatism. He believed the meaning of an idea lies in its practical consequences. Peirce emphasised how we gain knowledge through inquiry and experimentation.

John Dewey, another American philosopher, built on Peirce's ideas and became a leading figure in pragmatism. He stressed learning by doing and believed education should develop critical thinking and problem-solving, not just memorise facts. Dewey also saw democracy as essential to fairness and the common good.

Jürgen Habermas, a German philosopher, is known for his theory of communicative action and the 'lifeworld.' Habermas emphasised rational discourse and the public sphere as central to democracy and addressing social issues.

1.5 Academic Practitioners

In the overview of practitioner examples (figure 10), some professions require academic study and a master's degree in order to formally practice. For instance, to become an architect, doctor, or dentist, one must complete an academic education—and in the case of medicine, even further specialised training is needed for licensure.
Francis, for example, was educated in the tradition of industrial product design, a practice that can be studied both at academic universities and universities of applied sciences. I highlight this because practice-oriented academic programs like this are outnumbered by the traditional academic studies that focus on theory rather than on practice. In theoretical programs, students primarily learn to make decisions for the sake of understanding, modeling, or research, not necessarily for immediate application in real-world situations.
When academically trained individuals enter professional practice, for example when they start working in a business or in public administration, they must start making decisions that have direct consequences in the real world.
However, their education has typically prepared them with theoretical knowledge (knowing why), rather than the practical, intuitive knowledge of (knowing that).
Theory implicitly assumes decisions made in theory will hold up in practice. In theory, that might be true. But in practice, things are rarely so predictable. You can only forecast outcomes to a certain extent.

'That is an interesting point you are making', reflects James. 'When I studied Public Administration and Sociology, the research I learned to do indeed had the purpose of building theory, to describe the situation as it is. For example, for my thesis, I sent out a questionnaire to test some hypotheses I had based on literature research. Then I had to use the empirical data I gained from filled-out questionnaires to draw conclusions on my hypotheses, and of course, advice for further research. You know, I needed to showcase I was able to do academic work.'

'But I also remember when I just started working as a junior policy advisor', James goes on. 'I had no idea if what I was doing was the right thing to do. So, I asked my manager. He basically decided for me. Over the years, I developed a gut feeling for well-written and badly written policy advice and how to navigate my organisation. I learned decision-making on the job, not during my academic education.'

'I remember I had to design a kitchen appliance tool that would enhance the joy of cooking together', reflects Francis. 'I made the decision to focus on the father-daughter relationship, so dads and their little girls were my target audiences. I did solid research, observed seven households, and made this prototype of my product design, which I was quite proud of. It took me a lot of time to build. Then I visited some families at home to test my design. The first thing this five-year-old said was: what is that ugly thing? Then in the second family, the father told me he was sorry, but he would never use my product because it was too complicated to use. I was devastated. I almost quit my studies. After crying for a week, I pulled myself together and decided to change the entire thing, making a kitchen weight/counter product. The dad can set the weight or number of pieces needed. The daughter can throw it in, and when the number of pieces or weight is reached, a song plays. They loved it! I'll never forget it. Tough learning, but the best experience ever.'

'You actually went into their homes?' James asks, surprised.

'Of course', Francis replies.

'But how did you even find those people?' James continues.

'I asked around if any of my peers had an older sibling with kids. One did, and through him, I connected with a few other father-daughter pairs. Then, I reached out to a primary school to see if they could spread the word about my project. That effort got me three more pairs', Francis recalls.

'You really did all that?' James says, astonished.

'Why are you so surprised? If I wanted to make an informed decision about how to move forward, I needed real input from my target audience. So, I just figured out ways to reach them. It's not that difficult.' Francis is slightly puzzled by James' reaction.

'When I started as a junior policy advisor, I worked on projects about building a more Playful Society. But never once did it occur to me to simply grab my coat, go to a playground, and ask kids and parents for their thoughts. I never thought to visit the very places my policies would affect.'

'Why not? You were designing something meant to improve their lives. Wouldn't it make sense to talk to them?'

'It just wasn't how things were done. Maybe because no one else did it, so I didn't either. Or maybe because it felt too random—just because kids in one playground liked an idea, how could I know kids elsewhere would feel the same? Randomness does not fit with the idea of equal treatment. Besides, we had a thick report of research on the topic we could use.'

'Yeah, paper doesn't really give you a feel for the topic, does it?' Francis says decisively.

'What?' James looks up from his thoughts.

'Five playgrounds. That's my number. After five, a pattern starts to emerge. Sometimes, you see it after three. Other times, you need ten.'

'But that's time-consuming—and expensive.'

'Not as expensive as pushing forward with a plan that turns out to be unwanted. Then you've spent money and solved nothing. That's a lose-lose.'

'Not entirely lose-lose', James muses. 'If a minister promises playgrounds, they can at least show they kept

their promise—even if the playgrounds themselves fail.'
'That's ridiculous.'
'It's reality, but not really reality. Ministers aren't involved in something as small as playgrounds. That's usually a municipal issue.'

Being educated and working as a practitioner means making decisions and reflecting on them in real time, not in the safety of theory but in the unpredictable messiness of real life. It means feeling the pressure of choices as they unfold, bumping into constraints, and occasionally collecting a few bruises from unintended consequences. You can study it in theory, but true practitionership is like learning to swim—you only really get it once you're in the water, not just reading about the ocean from a dry chair.

Francis is educated to make design decisions by engaging directly with the design problem and adjusting ideas for solutions along the way in a constant loop of thinking (making decisions) and doing (acting upon those decisions). But within public administration, and other public organisations, decisions are often made elsewhere, by others, earlier, and far from the action.

2. Stability by Execution

2.1 Separation of Powers

James works in the public administration of a national government. While each democracy has its own quirks and structures, they all rest on a shared foundation: the separation of powers (see figure 11).

In this classic democratic setup, power is sensibly divided. Politicians make the decisions (legislative power), civil servants like James put them into action (executive power), and the judiciary keeps an eye on everyone to make sure things stay within the legal lines (judicial power). It's a system designed to balance power—and occasionally, blame.

Legislative Power

The legislative power consists of Parliament, Ministers, and—

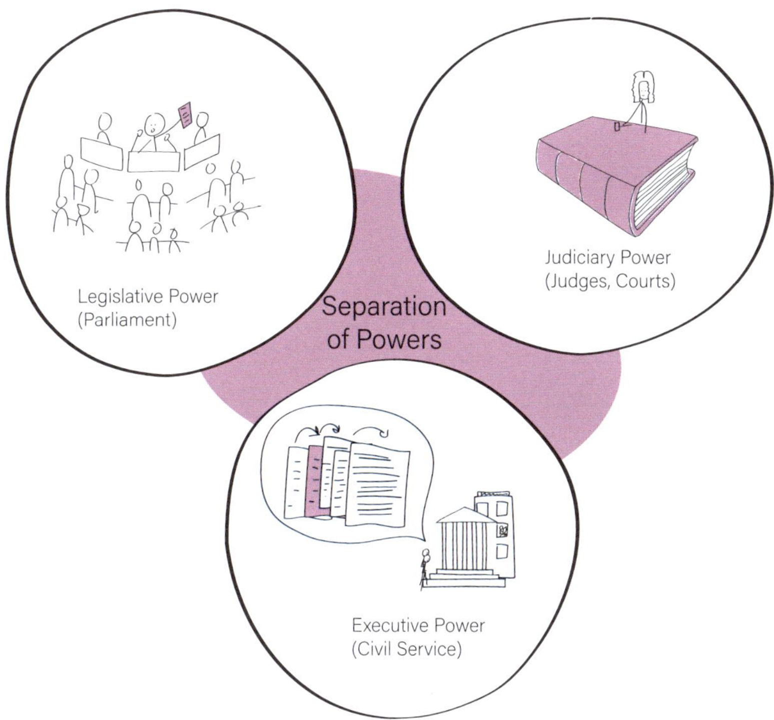

Figure 11: Separation of Powers.

in republics—the President. These individuals are (in)directly elected by the people and have the authority to make laws and decide how tax revenues are spent.

Judiciary Power

The judiciary is an independent branch of government. Although publicly funded, it operates free from political control. Courts and judges ensure that laws are applied correctly and that decisions made by Parliament or the President stay within legal boundaries.

Executive Power

The executive branch is the domain of the civil service. Civil servants advise Parliament, 'speak truth to power', and are responsible for implementing laws and policies. This is James's world.

Unlike politicians, civil servants are (supposed to be) politically neutral and remain in office regardless of elections. This stability allows them to take a long-term perspective. In his role as a policy advisor, James helps shape public policy in line with legal frameworks and legislative decisions.
To design within a government context is to design within this system. Most designers are not elected officials, so they typically work within or alongside the executive branch—often in collaboration with civil servants like James.

2.2 The Constitutional Tradition

The first tradition in governments, the constitutional tradition, emerged at the beginning of the twentieth century. The legitimacy of public administration is based on implementing the law, following rules and accountable procedures, to create predictable policies for citizens[27]. In this tradition, civil servants are to follow orders neutrally and rationally[28],

27 Wilson (1989), and Rothstein (2012).

28 Stout (2017), and Braams, et al. (2021).

not creatively[29]. Public administration has its foundation in a bureaucratic system.

Bureaucracy

In the early years of the previous century, you would receive better treatment if you were the nephew of the King than if you were the son of a farmer. Max Weber, the German sociologist, advocated for a more rational and fair system that supported equal treatment: a bureaucratic system. In this system, decisions should be made rationally based on rules, eliminating randomness. Weber also saw the advantage of separating politics from the organisations executing the laws through civil servants. As civil servants are not elected and (should not be) politically biased, they are 'neutral'. Bureaucracy was meant to create fair treatment for all citizens in a democratic system.
Max Weber famously warned that bureaucracy, while essential for fairness and order, can become a lifeless machine that limits individual freedom. When public administration operates like this machine, citizens may face frustrating red tape as they navigate rules and regulations just to access services they're entitled to. Yet, despite these drawbacks, bureaucracy remains a cornerstone of fair democracy.

Procedures: Means or Goals?

At the heart of bureaucracy are procedures designed to ensure

---

29 Torfing and Triantafillou (2016).

equal treatment. Civil servants must follow these procedures to guarantee that every case is handled consistently, predicting outcomes and creating stability (see figure 12). Success, in this context, is defined by adherence to rules rather than by the effectiveness of the outcome. When things go wrong, decision-makers can blame the rules rather than themselves. However, problems arise when procedures become ends in themselves rather than tools for achieving goals. This can lead

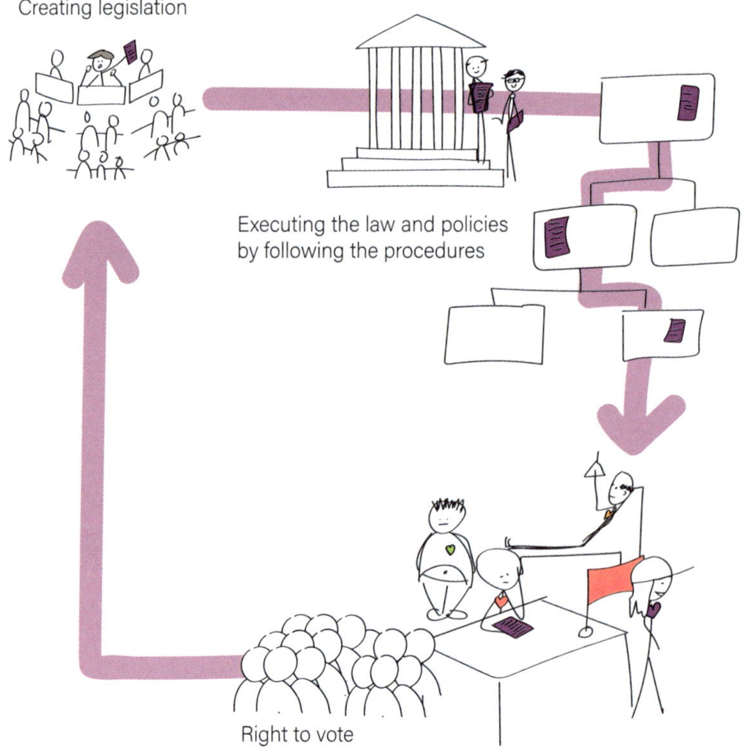

Figure 12: Representation of the constitutional tradition in public administration: focus on procedures.

to absurd situations, like a lamppost in the middle of a parking lot simply because 'the plan says so'. It's like a doctor claiming: 'The operation was a success because we followed all protocols. Unfortunately, the patient died.' Procedures were created to prevent favoritism, not to replace human judgment. Blind adherence to rules cannot justify unjust outcomes.

Stability

Because procedures emphasised predictability, fairness, and consistency, the civil service naturally favors stability over change. Its strength lies in creating a reliable, impartial system. But this same strength makes it resistant to react rapidly to (disruptive) change. Civil servants are guardians of continuity, which means change often comes slowly and cautiously within public administration.

'We have procedures for change', James smiles cynically. *'So, Francis, when you enter James' office, you can expect resistance.'*
'You put it really black and white, though', reflects James. 'It's not like we don't think and blindly follow procedures. Actually, as a policy-maker, I create procedures.'
'Of course, you think for yourself. I'm referring to the foundations of the system of executing governments. In the past century, layers of new ways of working entered the government, nuancing my argument above. Not only that, but also procedures have become highly

dependent on computer systems.'

The purpose of bureaucracy is efficiency, predictability, and change is not a friend of that system. No matter how much nuance you try to give to the situation. The tension is always there.

2.3 Taylorism

Bureaucracy is based on ideas from American mechanical engineer Frederick Winslow Taylor. In 1911, Taylor's work 'The Principles of Scientific Management' was published. Taylor advocated for the rational standardisation of production processes.

Work by Task Division

Taylor argued that by breaking down production into smaller, specialised tasks, efficiency could be significantly improved. The person responsible for designing the work (the thinking) was not the same as the person carrying it out (the doing) (see figure 13).

In 1911, during the height of the Industrial Revolution, this approach aligned well with the nature of work at the time. Factory labor was repetitive and mechanical, and most workers had little or no formal education. Their roles required following instructions rather than making decisions, and they were often treated as extensions of the machines they

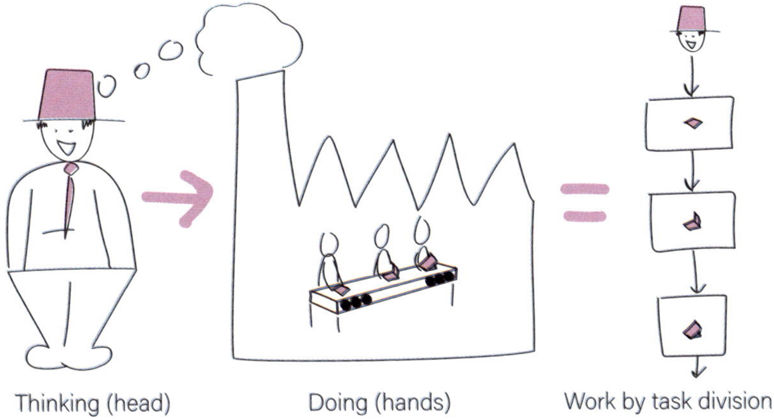

Figure 13: Work by task division.

operated. Given this context, Taylor's ideas fit the era well. His methods matched an industrial system built on standardisation and control—where it made sense to separate planning from execution and to treat labor as a predictable, machine-like process.

However, Taylor's idea of task division did not stay in the factory of the Industrial Revolution. For example, the American army adopted Taylor's ideas on management in their training programs in preparation for, and during World War II. But the chaos of the battlefield is different from the structure in the factory.

Planning and Control Cycles

The separation of decision-making and execution showcased too rigid an approach and proved problematic in the chaos of battle in World War II. For example, during the Battle of

Kasserine in North Africa, six American soldiers died for every one German soldier[30].
Instead of empowering soldiers with decision-making authority on the battlefield, like the Germans did, the army doubled down on detailed planning and strict adherence to those plans, leaving no room for individual initiative. This led to the development of the first planning and control cycles.
The reaction was: the more there is chaos, the more we need to control the chaos.
Planning and control cycles use a 3CI model: Command, Communication, Control, Intelligence. The Command is Communicated 'down.' Through Intelligence, the Commander keeps Control over the progress (see figure 14). Over the past century, Taylor's ideas have formed Western organisations and institutions.

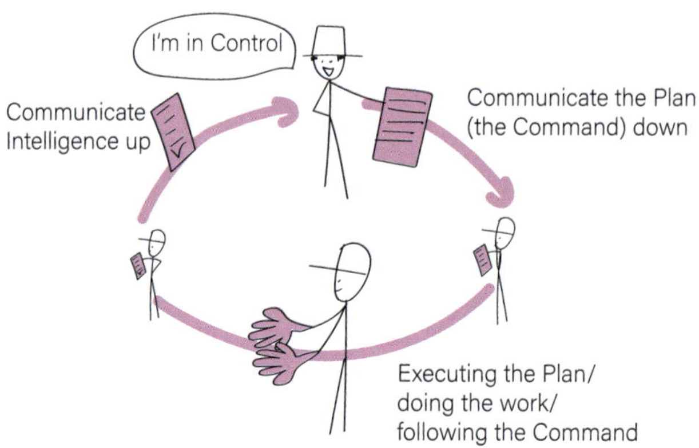

Figure 14: Control cycle.

30 Brouwer & Moerman (2005), page 62.

Best Kept Secret: Rhinish-way of Organising Work[31]

Anglo-American values and ideas have spread through Western societies in the past century. The way we organise work is one of those ideas. But historically, there are other ways used to organise work. There is very little written in organisational literature about the Rhinish-way of organising work. Organisational literature is overwhelmingly English dominated, with a distinct lack of European studies in comparison to their American and English counterparts[32].
The Rhinish-way of organising work flowed from a different form of capitalism, as described by Michel Albert in 'Capitalism contre Capitalism' (1991). Rhinish capitalism is rooted in the societies of countries like Germany, Switzerland, and the Netherlands[33], countries bordering the Rhine River, which was the border of the Roman Empire. Differences between Rhinish and Anglo-American capitalism are not based solely on economics but are deeply embedded in the institutional and cultural makeup of these societies.
Historically, Western European countries have placed greater emphasis on community and long-term stability, whereas Anglo-American societies have favored individual initiative and short-term gain. These macro-level cultural values influence the institutional structures at the meso-level—laws, insurance systems, education, and military organisation.

---

31 Brouwer & Moerman (2005), and Albert (1997; original 1991).

32 Meyer & Boxenbaum (2010).

33 Albert also refers to Scandinavia, and Japan. Cultural differences should be taken into account.

One institutional example is the legal systems. The civil law systems found in most European countries are derived from Roman law, emphasising comprehensive codes and consistent application of legal principles. This creates a high level of predictability and coherence, allowing individuals and organisations to understand their responsibilities and rights within a well-defined framework.
In contrast, common law systems in the UK and USA rely heavily on precedent and judicial interpretation. Laws evolve case by case, often resulting in legal complexity and frequent litigation. This contributes to a culture where legal expertise becomes a specialised competitive advantage.
Even in the realm of military organisation, these differences are apparent. In the 19th century, the German military developed a mission-oriented approach, empowering officers on the ground to make decisions within a clear strategic framework. This required soldiers to be highly trained, with strong integration of practical experience and theoretical knowledge. Decision-making was decentralised and informed by direct engagement with unfolding events. The American army, by contrast, applied a centralised model based on standardised procedures and strict hierarchy, reflecting the influence of Taylorism. Soldiers were expected to follow plans rather than adapt to changing circumstances.
These structural and cultural foundations give rise to different organising principles. The Anglo-American approach prioritises Command, Control, Communication, and Intelligence. The Rhinish model, also with a history of guild structures, centers on four guiding principles (see figure 15): **Practitionership**, which values expertise at the operational level; **Connectivity**, which emphasises real-world

interactions between people; **Trust**, which enables autonomy within a shared understanding; and **Inspiration**, to grow in practitionership.

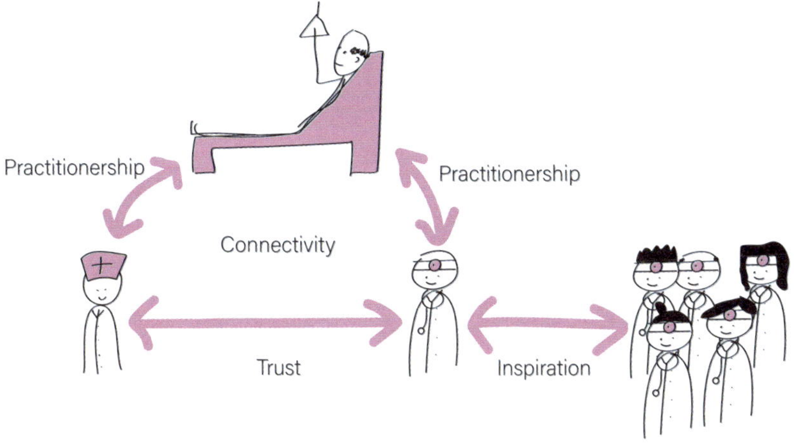

Figure 15: Guiding principles in Rhinish-way of organising

2.4 Taylor: A Ghost in the Machine

More than a century after Frederick Taylor introduced Scientific Management, it may feel quaint (if not uncomfortable) to think of workers as cogs in a machine. Today's jobs often demand complex judgment, empathy, or even academic-level problem-solving. Yet, the language we use to organise work hasn't kept pace.

We still speak of executing functions and feeding decisions back into the line, a nod to the old assembly line. Employees are referred to as 'Human Resources', a term that sounds more like fuel than people. We divide organisations into 'the head of a department' that does decision-making. And strangely, in most standard organisational charts, the client—supposedly the reason the organisation exists—is nowhere to be found (see figure 16). Taylor may be long gone, but his ghost is still with us.

Climbing the Ladder

Education systems often reinforce the split between thinking and doing. Academic achievement is held up as the gold standard, while practical education is valued as inferior.
We call it 'higher education', and it tends to lead to 'higher' positions, those involving less doing and more overseeing.
To 'move up' the career ladder usually means to stop doing the work and start managing those who do. This implies that to lead, you don't need to understand the substance of the work—just the system that delivers it. Managing becomes an abstract activity: organising spreadsheets, optimising KPIs, crafting processes from above.
But managing is not the same as doing, and understanding a process on paper doesn't mean you can lead it in practice. The assumption that decision-makers can rely solely on Command, Control, Communication, and Intelligence, without real content expertise, may lead to absurd outcomes: strategies that look perfect in theory but collapse in practice.
But *managing* or administrating business is not the same as *doing* business. When managers focus solely on spreadsheets and numbers, reality gets filtered through a theoretical lens. The numbers become more important than what's actually

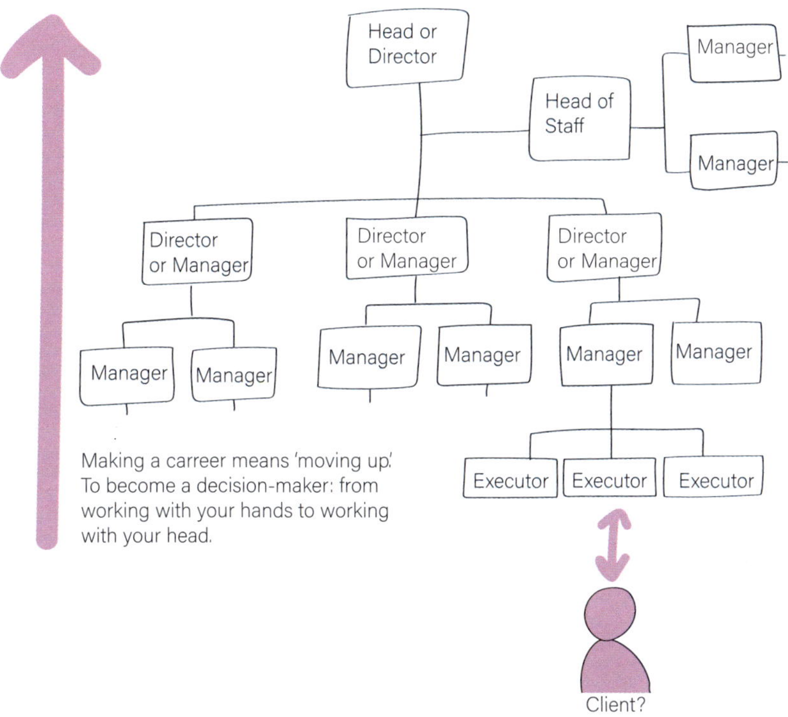

Figure 16: A normalised representation of an organisation.

happening. In extreme cases, what is true on paper, or on a computer screen, is accepted as true without common sense. As James reflected, when you learn to make decisions to build theory, it's difficult to keep an eye out for practice. Managers (decision-makers) create new procedures without testing them in real-world conditions. Implementation is just a mere formality. They expect employees to execute changes flawlessly, without considering whether they're practical, realistic, or even beneficial.

But as any experienced executor will tell you, practice rarely unfolds like a perfect business case. Moreover, complexity in execution has risen over the past century. Execution is not putting a lid on a pot in a production line; execution is the work of practitioners, especially in public services like health and education.

James put it, once you are educated, it's easy to forget how theories work out and what actually works. Developing new procedures that may look elegant on a screen, but they haven't been tested against reality. Implementation becomes a rubber stamp: just send it down the line and expect flawless execution.

2.5 Change in a Context of Stability

Public administration is built on principles of predictability and fairness. Bureaucracy needs to ensure that citizens are treated equally and that political decisions are implemented consistently. In this system, procedures are not just helpful, they are essential. They provide the framework for civil servants to do their jobs without bias and with accountability. When society changes, the very system designed to serve society is built to resist change. In other words, based on bureaucracy, the system tries to maintain stability by resisting change—but by doing so, it becomes increasingly unstable in a changing world.

Change in bureaucracy is perceived as a risk because it threatens the foundations of predictability; the outcome of a change is uncertain. Altering procedures, workflows, or systems creates the possibility that things won't go as planned. It is not the change in itself that is perceived as risky, but the uncertainty that creates the feeling of risk. In a political context, that unpredictability is deeply uncomfortable. A failed policy or poor implementation can have real political consequences, public criticism, media backlash, or even lost elections. To manage this discomfort, bureaucracies respond to uncertainty with more control: more detailed planning, more procedures, more approvals. Every possible 'what if' is mapped out before action is taken. The intention is to reduce uncertainty.

Uncertainty embraced, designers approach uncertainty as part of their practice. Even more so, designers are initiators of change by creating something new.

3. Designing vs. Governing

3.1 To change or Not to Change

From the foundations of designing and governing the constrast could not be greater. Designers, who embrace and initiate change, and government organisations, which are resistant and only change when change if forced upon the them.

Controlling vs. Anticipating

As uncertainty rises—an inherent characteristic of undertaking something new, the instinct is often to tighten control. However, the more rigid the procedures become, the less adaptable the system is. Plans can transform into constraints. Decision-making slows, and those closest to the operational realities, who possess the most accurate insights, are often the least empowered to deviate from the established plan.

This dynamic is exemplified by the presence of lanterns in the middle of parking lots rather than on sidewalks.
In civil service, when a situation does not conform to the established procedure, the decision escalates up the hierarchy, creating a backlog for managers. Their initial response is typically not to amend the procedures or distribute authority, as that would require considerable effort and time. Instead, they often opt to hire additional managers to manage the increasing volume of exceptions. Thus, heightened control becomes the solution to issues precipitated by excessive control.
Conversely, designers anticipate unpredictability; it is an intrinsic aspect of their practice. They experiment with new ideas in small settings to transform uncertainties into certainties. Yet, in a system that equates uncertainty with risk and risk with failure, even modest experiments can require extensive time for approval.

Who Makes the Decisions?

In the field of public administration, work is still fundamentally organised around an antiquated concept: the separation of responsibilities. The individual who decides does not execute. Designers, confronted not only by the complexities of governmental procedures but also by a surprisingly ambiguous question, often wonder: who truly makes the decision when innovation is required?
For designers, this question may seem trivial; their roles inherently involve the creation of new concepts. Each act of

creation necessitates decisions that have not been previously made. Thus, when a designer proposes a modification within the realm of public administration, who ultimately decides whether that modification will be implemented?
Decisions are typically made through formal procedures, which are often linked to hierarchical mandates. The focus is not on who possesses the most expertise, but rather on who is authorised to act. This distinction is not a minor technicality; within government, decision-making must also guarantee fairness, legality, and consistency for all citizens. Therefore, while a designer might advocate, 'Let us change this because it functions more effectively', a civil servant may counter, 'I require permission because this does not align with established procedures.' Consequently, designers accustomed to autonomy are compelled to persuade others, often those in higher positions, to make decisions that they themselves are prepared to undertake. Given that design decisions typically involve change rather than stability, resistance is a common occurrence.

The Expert or The Manager

When a designer lacks the expertise to make a specific decision, they do not seek guidance from someone higher in the hierarchy; instead, they consult an individual with the relevant knowledge. For instance, if an industrial product designer is uncertain about the required thickness of a plastic component to prevent breakage, she does not approach her manager for advice. Rather, she ensures that a materials

engineer is involved in the design process to help ascertain that the solution is sufficiently robust without being unnecessarily heavy. The expert is not merely a consultant but plays an integral role in the conception and development of the idea. Designers organise circular, like a network, instead of vertically (see figure 17).
Ironically, while designers possess strong creative problem-solving skills, they frequently lack the policy knowledge necessary to navigate the constraints of civil service. Thus, although they can envision improved methodologies, they are not positioned to make the necessary decisions. Conversely, those who are empowered to decide often lack the substantive expertise to assess whether the proposed design is sound. Ultimately, the issue lies not in the differentiation between thinking and doing, but in the separation of these roles among different individuals. When decision-making is removed from practical application, change becomes a purely theoretical

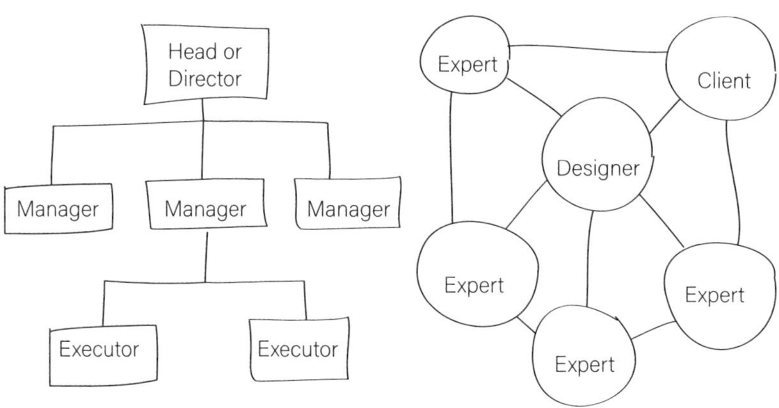

Figure 17: Vertical way of organising vs. a networked way of organising.

exercise. Conversely, when the practitioner also serves as the thinker—engaging in reflective practice—decisions can adapt to align with reality. This dynamic complicates the management of expert practitioners, as they do not conform to static plans due to their capacity to learn through action.
To foster change, it is imperative to allow for uncertainty. However, within most systems, the impulse to exert control over that uncertainty renders the creation of anything.

3.2 Inherited Baggage Foundations

Francis and James carry legacies in their backpacks. Page 71 summarises the values, beliefs, and ideas that define what is considered a good job, based on the foundations of design and governance. Pages 72–73 present an overview table of the inherited baggage, including the key principles that emerge from these legacies.

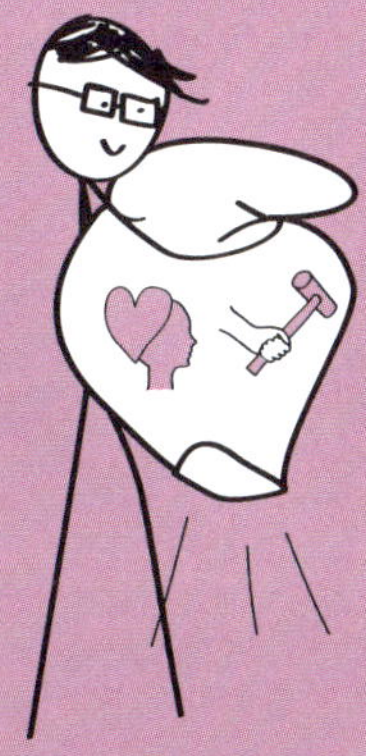

I execute the law.
I value equal treatment.
I believe it is good to follow procedures to ensure stability and equal treatment. Therefore, I believe that the person who, according to the procedure, makes the decisions should make those decisions.
I believe change is risky because change doesn't follow procedures.
I work according to the plan and adjust the plan where needed to realise the predefined objective.
I do a good job when I follow procedures and execute the law.

I have a practice.
I value creation.
I believe that change is good and that I can solve problems and fix things. I'm used to making decisions myself, based on my expertise and that of others.
I work iteratively; I see what evolves in front of me and steer accordingly. I use my hands as well as my head.
I do a good job when I'm satisfied with my practice. And that is when I create an idea and a plan for realisation, which – when realised – adheres to all criteria.

	Traditions in Public Administration	Leading principle in James' context	What is designed	Designed by	
FOUNDATIONS	**Stability by Execution <1980**		**Practionership of Creation**		
	Constitutional (bureaucracy)	Follow procedures to execute the law	Everything artifical: created by humans	Designer	
	Systemworld 1980-2000		**Lifeworld**		
	Collaboration 2000-2020		**Co-Creation**		
	Integration >2020 - Social Designers				

Overview Inherited Baggage

Leading principle in Francis' practice	Designed in the Context of (viability)	Designed for (desirability)	Design realised by (feasibility)
Change by creation by allround practionership (thinking + doing)	Depends on what is designed	Depends on what is designed	Depends on what is designed

Focus 1980-2000

In the early 1980s, a new tradition in public administration emerged. The discretionary tradition applied neoliberal business principles to civil service and emphasised organisational systems. The Systemworld James grew up with.
In the practice of industrial product designers, there is a strong focus on the Lifeworld. Designers are trained to understand people as consumers and create objects that interact with the Lifeworld, in the realm of human experience. Wicked Problems could have bridged these two worlds, but the time wasn't yet right.

4. Systemworld

4.1 Lead up to Neoliberalism

Wicked problems. Each argument in favour of using a 'designerly approach' for societal challenges begins with it. The 'wicked problem' was popularised in design theory by Horst Rittel & Melvin Webber, an urban planner and an architect.
At the beginning of the 1990s, industrial product design scholar Richard Buchanan brought the concept into the design discipline of industrial product design.
Rittel & Webber's seminal paper, called 'Dilemmas in a General Theory of Planning', describing wicked problems, was published in the academic Journal of Policy Sciences as early as 1973.
Rittel & Webber (1973) open their article with the dissatisfaction felt by the American population in society at that time. America in the 1970s was indeed not doing very well[34], neoliberalism was the answer. However, a few decades earlier,

34 Albert (1997; orginal 1991).

the Americans were on top of the world! What happened?

America from WWII to 1980 in a Nutshell[21]

Einstein moved to America in 1933 when Hitler came to power in Germany. Many other scientists and philosophers did the same. America took over the role of hub of Western knowledge and the country flourished after they got rid of Hitler. Along with the British and the Canadians, they were seen as 'great liberators' from Hitler's terror. By the end of WWII, America's dominant position was solidified with the establishment of the Bretton Woods system. During the conference in 1944 (in Bretton Woods), an international agreement was reached on fixed exchange rates for currencies. It was the first international monetary system. The system was fairly straightforward—one currency could be exchanged for another, but only American dollars could be exchanged for gold (see figure 18).

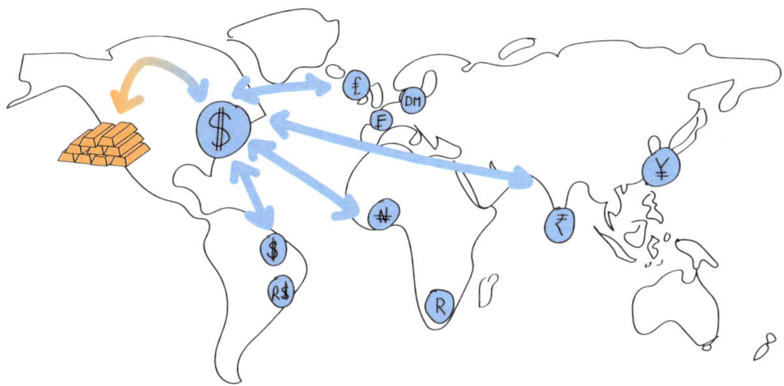

Figure 18: Bretton Woods system.

The International Monetary Fund (IMF) was established to manage currency fluctuations, while the World Bank was tasked with aiding economic development and reconstruction programs.
The USA became a great power, possessing 50% of the world's gold, leading in technological processes, and accounting for half of the world's industrial production.
Thirty-one years after the establishment of the Bretton Woods system, Nixon pulled the plug on August 15, 1971, announcing that the dollar would no longer be tied to gold. The dollar lost a whopping 80%(!) of its value in a single day.

Failure of the Bretton Woods System

The Bretton Woods system failed due to internal contradictions. On the one hand, America was tasked with keeping the dollar stable since it was the primary international trading currency, creating a constant demand for US dollars. On the other hand, domestic politics sometimes benefited from having fewer dollars in circulation. The point came when four times as many dollars were in circulation as the value of the gold they represented!
Due to significant trade deficits, especially exacerbated by the Vietnam War, US inflation soared, weakening the country's international competitiveness. Other nations wanted to exchange their dollars for gold, losing faith in the US's ability to maintain order. But there were too many dollars going around and too little gold to represent those dollars, leading to Nixon's decision.

With the failure of the Bretton Woods system, money itself became a commodity. Money no longer represented something tangible like gold; its value was determined by the market, much like sugar or milk or even entire companies, as we have witnessed.
So, in the early 1970s, when Rittel & Webber wrote their article, dissatisfaction with professionalism in public services or public education came from the citizens who would like to see things differently, but also from the professionals themselves.

Predictability & Arrogance[35]

According to Rittel & Webber, the efficiency gained through automation since the industrial revolution works for engineering problems and also for (urban) planning problems because consensus was fairly easy to achieve, and then you could ask someone with technological skill to execute the solution to a problem. But societies have increased in complexity. By the 1970s, Rittel & Webber concluded that you cannot predict the outcome of a new neighborhood the way you can predict the strength of a wall. Urban planning may result in bricks and stones, but the criteria that need to be taken into account are not lifeless. We are dealing with social constructs, groups of humans that live somewhere, move around, have feelings, and behave in unpredictable ways. They even call it arrogant to think we can problem-solve our way

---

35 Rittel & Webber (1973).

through societal planning issues.
They argue that you cannot pinpoint a societal problem to one cause. There are interdependencies. For example, poverty and obesity are related, or the way streets are designed and the greenery in the neighborhood are related to crime rates. These types of problems are 'wicked.'

4.2 Defining Wicked Problems

Wicked problems are ill-defined and actually cannot be solved but only dealt with or resolved. That makes the term wicked *problem* unfortunate because a problem is defined by the fact that it is solvable. If not, we are dealing with a situation or a challenge rather than a problem. But anyway, the fact that wicked problems are ill-defined means they can be defined in several ways, depending on the perspective you take.
Take the societal problem of obesity, for example. If you work for a health department, you look for (re)solutions in terms of getting people to exercise more, so maybe you want to subsidise sports memberships. If you work in the Ministry of Social Security, you might want to educate people about food or create programs to decrease poverty. If you work in the Ministry of Education, you might want to arrange more exercise in schools and education about healthy food. Although both ministries are part of the same government, job positions influence perspectives, which influence the mental space in which you search for a 'solution'.

10 charactistics of Wicked Problem[36]

1. **No clear definition**: wicked problems can't be neatly defined; how you frame the problem is closely tied to the solution you propose.
2. **No clear end point**: there's no objective point at which you can say the problem has been definitively solved.
3. **Solutions are subjective**: solutions aren't right or wrong. They can only be judged as better or worse, depending on context and values.
4. **No standard method**: there is no universal set of procedures or tools that guarantee a solution.
5. **Multiple interpretations**: wicked problems can be understood in various ways, often shaped by one's worldview, background, or discipline.
6. **Part of a bigger issue**: they are often symptoms of more complex, underlying problems.
7. **No clear test of success**: there's no conclusive way to evaluate whether a proposed solution truly works.
8. **One-shot attempts**: each intervention alters the situation in irreversible ways. There's no opportunity to test and revise.
9. **Uniqueness**: every wicked problem is distinct; past solutions can't simply be reapplied.
10. **Full accountability**: The person or team addressing the problem is fully responsible for the consequences of their actions, there's no one else to blame.

---

36 Buchanon (1992).

Criteria for the solution depend on who is creating the criteria. An obese person will have different criteria for a good solution than the Minister of Health, the civil servant making policy, the trainer of a fitness club, the liposuction surgeon, or any random citizen.

These people have different experiences, different stakes, and so they have a different perspective on the situation: they would 'frame the problem differently' (see figure 19).

Figure 19: Looking at the same thing and seeing something different.

There is not one definition of the problem, and there is not a universal good answer to the problem, not one solution. Moreover, each solution will eventually lead to another problem. To 'solve' obesity, we need to consider interdependence and therefore take a systems approach to wicked problems.

Solutions for wicked problems are also difficult to test in lab situations. We can prototype a product or machine. But prototyping a 'solution' for obesity is not a simple tri-

al-and-error process. In Rittel & Webber's words[37]: *'[...] every implemented solution is consequential. It leaves 'traces' that cannot be undone. One cannot build a freeway to see how it works and then easily correct it after unsatisfactory performance.'* It is like testing a new curriculum for education. For the students receiving the 'test', it is the real deal.
Their article is a seminal piece of work in design theory; as I said, design scholars refer to them as the saviors of the discipline. Rittel & Webber could not have predicted that exactly the opposite of their argument became reality.

4.3 The Discretionary Tradition

Reagan and Thatcher

The American Dream, tarnished by the setbacks of the 1970s, became an 'American Disease.' The silent majority longed nostalgically for certainties and a return to traditional values, to the time when America was great and powerful.
On May 4, 1979, Margaret Thatcher was elected Prime Minister of Great Britain. Exactly half a year later, on November 4, 1980, Ronald Reagan was elected President of America. It marked the beginning of the era of Anglo-American capitalism and neoliberal societies.
So, Reagan boldly proclaimed: America is back! A rhetoric echoed by Trump's 'Making America Great Again', which led

37 Rittel & Webber (1973), page 163.

Trump to victory in the 2016 US presidential election and 'America First' in 2024. A rhetoric that is also gaining ground in European countries, where the sentiment of 'the people' is that yesterday was better than tomorrow will be.
Reagan introduced the Strategic Defense Initiative, aiming to end humiliation on the world stage. The logic? The bigger the army, the less likely the war! Oh, the paradox. Yet, it did spur a technological leap that helped 'win' the Cold War, thereby declaring capitalism victorious over communism: America is back! Thus, what he was doing looked successful; it seemed as if he was fulfilling his election promise.

> 'They have been tricked by the illusion of power, and by the power of illusion'[38]

Reagan's economic policy was like cutting the cheese: it smelled strong and left a lasting impression. By trimming spending on social programs, he showed confidence in welfare while beefing up defense spending to flaunt America's strength. Again, it looked fantastic! Reagan, the actor, looked fantastic too. He was even called The Great Communicator. The whole world bought into it. First Europe, then Africa, began to change the 'rules of the game' by privatising social services like energy, health, and public transport, thereby shifting focus to market competition and adhering to American

38 Albert (1997; orginal 1991), page 37.

values, also in the public domain[39]. With the fall of the Berlin Wall, capitalism prevailed over communism, and the 'Age of Neoliberalism' was born, along with a new governmental tradition that emerged in Western governments: discretionary tradition.

The Market Rules

In the context of the birth of neoliberalism, the discretionary tradition[40] took hold in public administration. In countries that had a tradition of public services being owned by the state, a new era began in which public services became private organisations and were subjected to market competition. The attractiveness lies in the idea that citizens get to choose their services.

The idea was that privatisation would lead to more efficient governments because the market would lead to an ideal and balanced situation. This concept stems from the beginning of capitalism, with Adam Smith during the period of the Enlightenment. The theory is that markets are self-controlling, like nature. People will take what they can without harming others, similar to trees taking up space but leaving room for other trees as well. However, people turn out to behave differently from trees.

Deregulation, privatisation, and centralisation were expected to create a faster and more efficient government than the

39 Albert (1997; orginal 1991).

40 Braams et al. (2021), and Stout (2017).

constitutional government. That idea backfired. To have private organisations execute public services, the government needs to organise that system, which creates new rules and regulations. By the mid-1990s, scholars concluded that the efficiency assumption was incorrect[41].

The discretionary tradition led to the norm that more control is the only way to manage expenses on civil services and that administration is important. The Command Control Communication Intelligence credo was strengthened even further.

Loosing and regaining control

When public service execution was outsourced to the market[42], governments lost control over the execution procedures and the results. Decision-makers in public administration could have responded in several ways. They could have accepted that you cannot control everything and left decision-making to the people who are 'on the battlefield', trusting them to do a good job, and accepting that societal problems are wicked, and that it is arrogant—in the words of Rittel & Webber—to control and try to predict outcomes of the future.

Alternatively, they could try to control whatever they could

41 Peters (1994).

42 In some countries, public services were never part of public administration. For example, healthcare insurances used to be part of public administration in the Netherlands, but that was not the case in the USA, where healthcare insurance was already a commercial activity.

control, creating a system in which procedural decision-making could remain intact. It may be of no surprise that governments working in a constitutional tradition leaned into the second option. Automation and computer technology also created opportunities to feel more in control.

Hollow State[28]

With the idea that societal issues are best left for the market to deal with, it leads to what public administration scholars call a 'Hollow State.' Public services that are no longer executed by the government but by the market lead to the impression that executing these services will cost less tax money. And it leads to the question: if services are executed by the market, what then is the job of the civil servant? What is the legitimacy of having a civil service? In public administration, this effect is referred to as the Hollow State.

Hospital Beds

For example, in country A, hospitals receive money from the government based on all sorts of quantitative measures, like how many beds the hospital has and what percentage of those beds are filled with patients. A better result is when most beds are filled because that is an efficient use of hospital beds. Because of automation, keeping track of the percentage of beds filled seemed easy peasy. Doctors monitor their patients anyway, and using software tools seems to save time.
So, a hospital buys the software, and every quarter they send this status to the government. But wait: to what entity of the

FOCUS

government? A new procedure needed to be created. And so, an administrative body in the Ministry of Healthcare takes on an accountant to keep track of the number of patients and, thereby, the entitled funds from all hospitals in the country. But hospitals also need to adhere to quality standards, safety standards, cleanliness standards, etc. For safety standards, floors in the hospital's kitchen need to hold a little ripple, making slipping more difficult. For hygienic reasons, the same floor needs to be flat so that no bacteria may grow in the corners of the floor tiles. Now what?

By the way, making money from a public service creates internal friction in a public organisation. The goal of the hospital is to help people get better, and receiving money for filled beds creates the opposite incentive of keeping patients in their beds.
And the competition it creates between hospitals to get their beds filled. Hospitals need to attract 'clients' (not patients); a marketer is hired to create a brand for the hospital. The money going to other activities besides the core task of a hospital increases.

With a growing possibility in the use of software controlling systems, a sense of control over results was created for all sorts of organisations.
The irony is that the efficiency that was supposed to be achieved by outsourcing public services was diminished by the new administrative controlling procedures designed to

give government a sense of control over the results. Since governments are strongly focused on procedures, with the good intention of equal treatment, these controlling procedures became more important than executing the public service: in other words, the focus on the organisational system increased.

The Responsibility Issue

These controlling procedures also 'solved' the problem of responsibility. When public services were outsourced, the legitimacy of governments came into question. Who then is responsible for them: the government or the public service providers? The controlling procedures give governments the illusion that they are retaining responsibility for their citizens. They provide the civil service with a reason for existence. The hospital with the beds and the kitchen floor is quite a simple example. Just take a moment to consider all the procedures that need to be in place when public administration needs to fund and control private organisations. The procedures must ensure that public sector organisations receive fair market treatment from the government and that citizens receive equal services.

'You make it sound as if it were the wrong choice to go for privatisation', reflects James.
'We will never know. But I do believe that the caution Webber had with bureaucracy was a prediction of the future. The leading principle of 'follow the procedure',

combined with outsourcing and market-based control of public services, may not have been the most effective approach. However, as the population grew and technology advanced, sticking to the way things were would also not make sense. Society changes. Governments are the backbone of society. When society bends one way, the government will also have to bend. You cannot keep doing the same thing but on a larger scale. As entrepreneurs know, scaling linearly is a death sentence.'

'What do you mean by that?' asks Francis.

'Imagine you're making dinner, and a friend spontaneously stays over. No problem, you throw in an extra portion. Now, three friends show up. You might make a quick supermarket run and decide on a special dish. Still manageable.

But what if ten friends come? Now, you need to plan ahead, borrow some chairs, and carefully choose a meal that works for a crowd. Thirty friends? You might resort to a buffet. And when a hundred people show up? Your house is useless—you need a whole new location. This dinner party scenario mirrors how society grows and evolves. You can't just do the same thing at a larger scale; you need new approaches. Scaling requires adaptation, not just repetition. Whether it's dinner parties or national policies, blindly applying the same logic at a larger scale rarely works.'

When societies expanded and technology advanced, old procedures became inadequate. Automation promised efficiency, but it also introduced rigidity. The more dependent we became on automated systems, the harder it was to adapt when change was needed.

4.4 Spreadsheet Becomes the Map

The rise of administrative control in the public sector started innocently, like hiring an accountant to control the efficiency of hospital beds. But since the 1980s, the logic of accountability has grown into a full-blown Systemworld—the world of the public administration organisations—, where every policy decision must be justified with predictions, business cases, and measurable outcomes. In this model, a public project is only approved if it can first prove its worth, worth on paper, that is. This sounds rational: why invest tax money without knowing what you'll get in return? But here's the catch: the need for upfront certainty leads to decision-making based on forecasts, not practice. Once a project is underway, success is no longer something experienced, but something reported. If the numbers say it worked, then it worked, regardless of what actually happened. Paper doesn't blush.
Take the 2016 decentralisation of Dutch youth care. Costs shifted to municipalities, conveniently disappearing from the national budget. It looked great on the financial spreadsheet. But in reality, municipalities struggled, and care quality

faltered. The numbers were neat, but the kids were not helped.

Practitioners Become Executors

As public services became 'private professionalised organisations' with business models, practitioners like general practitioners and teachers were repositioned: no longer autonomous professionals, but executing functions within a hierarchy (see figure 20). Decision-making moved upwards and was taken away from practitioners.

Meanwhile, the design world was having a different conversation. Rittel & Webber introduced the idea of Wicked Problems. Oddly enough, policy-making largely ignored

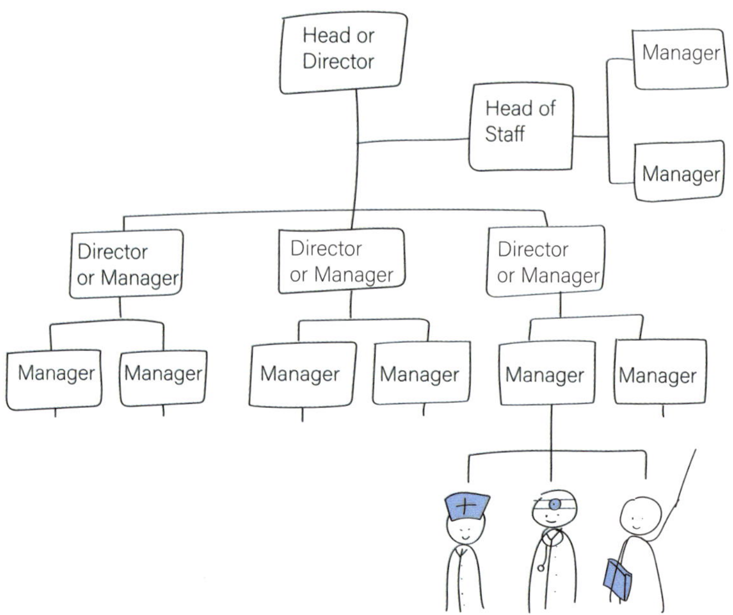

Figure 20: Practitioners in executing positions.

FOCUS

this complexity, instead em-bracing the idea of business administration as a way to control complexity.

Ironically, the discipline that truly embraced Wicked Problems wasn't urban planning or governance, where it arguably be-longed, but industrial product design. Why?

Because industrial product designers focus on consumers. They are educated to deal with the complexity of the Lifeworld: how people actually live, behave, love, and irrationally make decisions; not just the Systemworld of rational processes and Key Performance Indicators. Social designers who were educated in the legacy of Industrial Product Design have internalised this focus in their practice.

In a world where the map is mistaken for the terrain, we risk navigating policy with a compass made of numbers and wishful thinking. After all, if your GPS tells you you've arrived at your destination, but you're standing in a field with cows, maybe it's time to look up from the screen. And by the 2000s, civil servant started to look up from their screens, into the Lifeworld.

5. Lifeworld

5.1 Industrial Product Design

Emergence of the Discipline

Industrial Product Design became a design discipline[43] after World War II due to a combination of technological advancements and economic growth. The term 'Industrial Product' refers to the WHAT that is designed: a product that can be produced by machines.
Technological advancements have skyrocketed since the beginning of the Industrial Revolution. The discipline of Industrial Product Design wouldn't exist without the technological possibilities that allow humans to mass-produce products using machines. Industrial Product Design focuses on designing products that can be produced in large quantities in factories. But why produce in large quantities? The answer lies in mass consumption: we want a large number of people to buy these products.

43 A discipline is a field to study, educate in, and practice.

After World War II, mass consumption took off in the 1950s. More and more people in the West were able to afford luxury products. This created business opportunities, competition, and a demand for desirable products. The market for new products grew, leading to an increased need for industrial product design engineers. This resulted in Industrial Product Design becoming a design discipline in its own right.

The outcome of industrial product designing is a **tangible object** that can be **mass-produced**.

The Need to Dig Deeper

As Western societies grew wealthier, the problem-solving approach began to change. With rising incomes, people could buy more and more products, and soon markets became saturated. Every household already owned items like stick mixers, and competitors quickly copied and improved existing designs. Companies faced a critical question: what's next?
To stay in business, companies needed to innovate—not just by improving existing products but by creating entirely new ones. Consequently, industrial product designers tried to uncover problems consumers did not even realise they had to create demand for products that had not existed before. The focus shifted from problem-solving to problem-finding. 'What lies behind consumer behaviour? What implicit or latent problems could we solve with a product?' are questions that gained traction. By uncovering these hidden needs, companies could

create products that sparked a 'why didn't this exist before?' reaction and secure their place in a saturated market or create whole new markets altogether.

The Underlying Presumption of 'New is Better'

The core purpose of industrial product design has traditionally been (and in many cases still is) to persuade consumers to buy products. The practice is embedded in an industry that thrives on a constant stream of new offerings. As a result, industrial product designers are trained to focus on 'what's next.' They are always scanning for consumer pains and unmet needs because the status quo doesn't sell: if things are fine the way they are, there's no reason for a new product.

This drive for novelty may sit uncomfortably with designers who aim to contribute to the common good. The mass-production ethos—always more, faster, newer—probably doesn't align with the values of social designers, who are often more interested in meaningful change than in maximising consumption. But this characteristic of the 'mass-producible tangible object for consumers' has shaped a form of practitionership that pays close attention to real-world needs. Social designers educated in this tradition bring with them practice that, though born in the market, can offer valuable tools in the realm of governance.

5.2 The Industrial Product Designer's Paradox

Industrial product design engineers work at the intersection of three perspectives. First, the consumer perspective: will this be something people actually want to buy and use? Second, there's the business perspective: will the return on investment for whatever we create be positive? And third, the production perspective: can we realistically engineer and manufacture it? These three factors (see figure 21) are often referred to by the popular terms Viability (business), Desirability (consumer), and Feasibility (technology/engineering).
Understanding and overcoming the paradox between what makes sense financially, what appeals to users, and what is technically possible in the form of a product forms the core of the practice of industrial product designers.

> Industrial product designing: from identifying consumer needs, business opportunities, and technological possibilities, to ideating and developing the product, production, and market implementation.

In other words, the job of the industrial product designer is to synthesise these competing criteria into a single coherent product. Where others might see conflicting demands, designers work to create solutions that hold all three together.

The fact that industrial product designers need to incorporate consumer needs makes them focused on the Lifeworld[44].

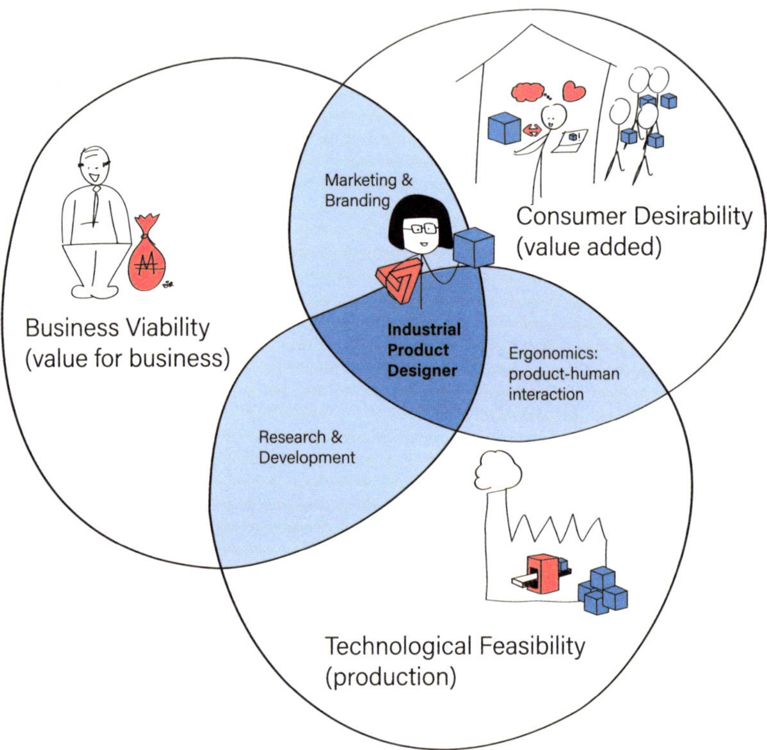

Figure 21: Three factors of Industrial Product Designing. Industrial product designers can be found in R&D departments, in Marketing & Branding jobs, or in ergonomics to research and test human-product interactions.

44 I'm freely borrowing the term Lifeworld from Habermas to describe the world outside the system of the organisation. The world we live in, in which we have our experiences. I would say reality, but system reality is also real.

5.3 Practitionership from this Legacy

Consumers as a Unique Starting Point

In the business-to-consumer (B2C) world, a consumer is someone who buys a product or service for personal use. Simple enough. But in a business-to-business (B2B) context, your buyer is a client—not someone who picks up a single item from a shelf, but someone who might order thousands or even millions of your product at once (see figure 22).
This difference changes the game entirely. If one client is buying in bulk, it's worth investing in a relationship—whether

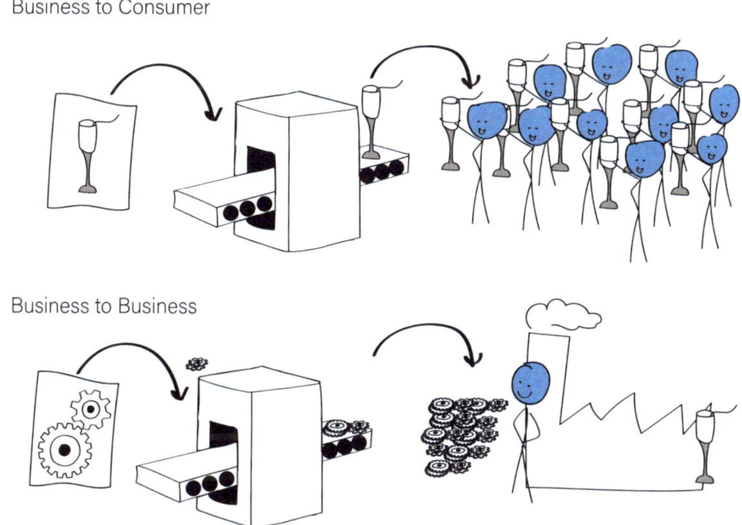

Figure 22: One thousand consumers buy one stickmixer, one client buys one thousands gears.

that means understanding their specific needs or, if you're like Vernon Dudley[45], letting them win at golf (wink). When one buyer holds the keys to a massive order, tailoring the product to their needs just makes sense.

Now contrast that with designing for the mass market. You're not going to have dinner with every single customer (unless you open a very ambitious restaurant). Each consumer has slightly different preferences, and understanding all of them individually is impossible.

That's why industrial product designers use a different approach. First, they search for shared needs across groups of people. They dig into real-life behaviour, frustrations, and unmet desires to uncover what's missing or could be better. Then, second, they are creative and come up with ideas, sketches, and models in order to test their ideas with smaller groups who share those needs. By gathering feedback and adjusting along the way, designers can validate whether their assumptions were right and improve their solutions before going to market.

This dual process of discovering needs and validating ideas for meeting those needs reduces the risk of launching a product that not enough people want to buy.

A Consumer Turned Out to Be a Person

From student to seasoned professional, every industrial product designer has faced the humbling—and strangely

45 If you don't know Vernon Dudley, you are obviously not a Harry Potter fan.

beautiful—moment when their brilliant idea completely misses the mark. The product they thought was elegant is dismissed as ugly. What seemed intuitive turns out to be confusing. What they were sure would be useful is met with indifference, or worse, frustration.

These moments are part of a designer's rite of passage. They reveal something fundamental: consumers are not abstract data points or personas on a slide. They're people. Real people. People with messy lives, who are worried about getting dinner on the table, picking up their kids, or trying to fix that one door that never closes properly. People who don't behave according to your blueprint, and whose needs are shaped as much by emotion as by reason.

This is what it means to design in the Lifeworld, the everyday world of lived experience, where habits, feelings, misunderstandings, and small annoyances rule. And in that world, even the best-laid design on paper can collapse under the weight of actual use.

This explains why industrial product designers are so deeply grounded in the Lifeworld. Their professional instinct is to test, tweak, and observe, not because they distrust their own ideas, but because they've learned not to trust the gap between intention and outcome. They don't assume a design will work just because it makes sense in theory. They know that reality is not a tidy machine: it's a person.

Practitionership: Connecting Worlds

Like most practitioners, industrial product designers are deeply connected to the Lifeworld. Unlike a doctor or a teacher, industrial product designers deliver their value indirectly. A doctor has direct contact with their patient, and a teacher with their student. Their activities take place in direct contact with the Lifeworld. An industrial product designer adds value through a product (see figure 23).

Figure 23: Industrial product designers deliver value through a product.

Unlike a doctor, whose activities take shape in the Lifeworld, industrial product designers also engage in activities that focus on the Systemworld and the Artificialworld (see figure 24). Their form of practitioners is not only forged through encounters with the unpredictable, emotional, and deeply human side of using products but also by adhering to criteria from business and physics. Their practitionership has created a mindset that holds value far beyond the product design studio, especially in domains like governance, where the Lifeworld and the Systemworld are often painfully out of sync. Industrial product designers developed this practitioner mindset through the search for latent consumer needs—those underlying, often invisible problems that shape people's behaviour. This approach naturally resonated with the idea of uncovering root causes in complex societal issues. So when Wicked Problems entered the design discourse, they felt familiar. Designers were already accustomed to working with contradictory demands, shifting contexts, and unpredictable human response characteristics that are also present in Wicked Problems.

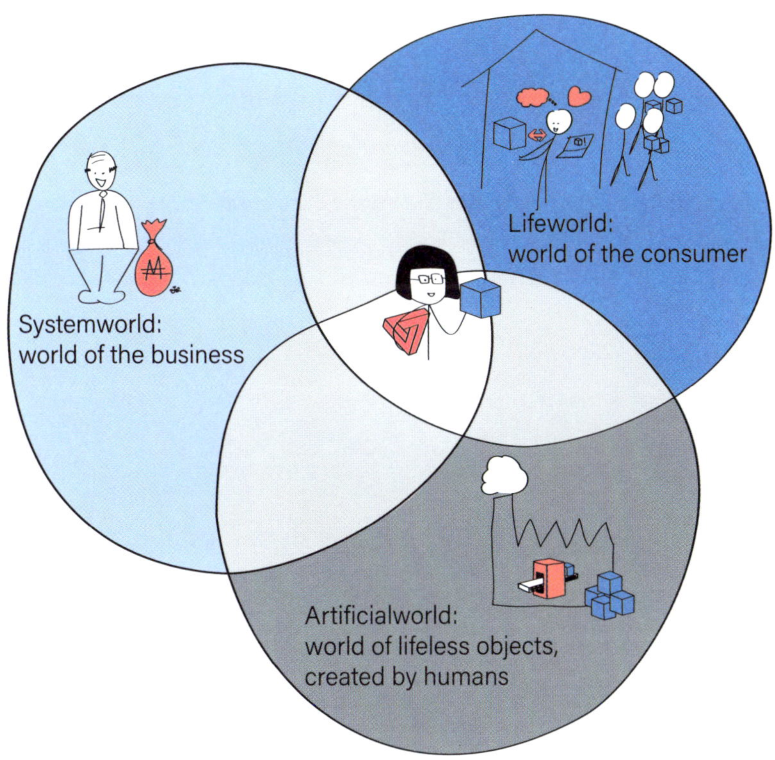

Figure 24: Practitionership of connecting worlds.

FOCUS

6.

Arrogance and Ignorance

6.1 Lifeworld & Systemworld Focus

Rittel & Webber called it arrogant: the way governments reduced complex societal issues to single, solvable problems. These issues were never singular. They were woven from unclear, shifting interdependencies. But in the 1980s, business language entered ministries, leading to a growing emphasis on control, measurable results, and internal accountability. This increased the focus on the system: reality on paper or on the computer screen. The introduction of digital technologies in public administration led to more efficiency at first but also reduced flexibility.

Industrial product designers also had to deal with something less predictable than any material: people. They had learned, sometimes painfully, that people do not behave as systems predict. What seemed like a good idea on the drawing board could be rejected outright in the Lifeworld. Products were misunderstood, ignored, or found ugly. Consumers were not rational actors in a model. They were (and are) busy humans, juggling daily lives, emotions, and frustrations. This taught designers a kind of humility. They developed a deep respect for the Lifeworld: how things actually play out in the hands and homes of real people.

But while they knew the Lifeworld of people, they didn't yet know the system world of public administration. Their education and practice were rooted in industry—serving markets, not public missions. So when some of these designers found themselves working on public issues, their legacy showed. They brought a rich understanding of people as consumers and users of products, along with creativity and decision-making abilities, but were often unaware of the organisational histories, values, and internal logics of the public institutions they were entering. In that sense, they carried a form of systemic ignorance.

Designers entering this world brought a much-needed sensitivity to the Lifeworld but lacked fluency in the system world. Their ways of doing clashed with the bureaucratic machinery built to protect consistency and control.

And even though it is not the end of the story, the situation described is still present. Figure 25 showcases the discreationary tradition in public administration, with a visual distinction between the Lifeworld and the Systemworld.

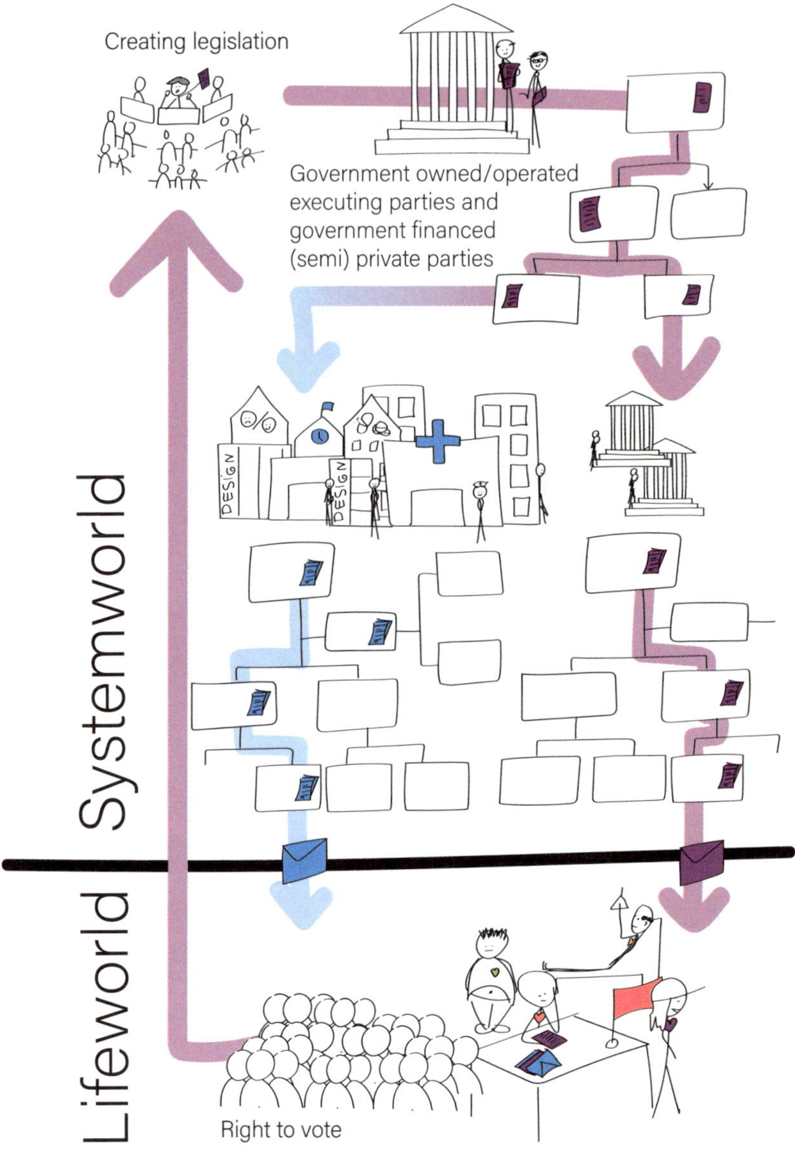

Figure 25: Representation of the discretionary tradition including the concepts of Lifeworld and Systemworld.

Predefined Goals and the Need to Dig Deeper

I'm sorry, I just can't get over something you said earlier, Francis', says James.

'That's okay, you can interrupt.'

'Francis, you mentioned that you change the objective mid-process?' recalls James.

'Yes, if we learn something valuable.' responds Francis.

'I just don't see how that is possible. How can you ensure adherence to the budget if you keep altering objectives?'

'I think you associate the term 'objective' differently than I do. I define an objective as a solution to a need. My ultimate goal is to fulfill that need. My focus is on the problem—because I have to make sure that my solution actually solves a problem, so people will pay for it. If I come up with a solution that doesn't work, I can change it', Francis explains.

'Right', James reflects. 'My objectives are dictated from above. There's not much room to 'change objectives'. Only once solutions are presented and a business case is approved can we initiate a project. During the project, we can't deviate much from the predefined objective, because that wasn't approved.'

'Yet when reality diverges from your plan, you do not adhere strictly, do you?' Francis inquires in disbelief.

'This tension constitutes a significant portion of my daily responsibilities. Can we adhere to the plan, or must we deviate? Do we require a new decision to amend the plan, and is the goal still attainable? At times, we must navigate commitments made by our Minister to Parliament, and when our Minister advocates for a particular policy, we are obligated to execute it as long as it remains within legal boundaries. We may not concur with the policy, but these internal ethical conflicts persist.'

'Perhaps you could ask yourself, 'How do we know if this solution actually solves the problem?' and try to frame it in a more problem-focused way', suggests Francis.

'This paradox is one of the dilemmas in change initiatives. How can you know what a change will deliver? It is not there yet. On the other hand, how can you secure funding to change something if you don't yet know what it will deliver—what the business case will be? The paradox may be solvable by choosing a higher level of abstraction to formulate an objective. Francis defines objectives as problems to be solved, not solutions to be executed. But James is in a situation where the solution is presented to him and he is obliged to execute it—noting that wicked problems can't be solved, only dealt with.'

6.2 Inherited Baggage Focus

Page 109 summarises the inherited baggage from the focus on the discretionary tradition and the discipline of Industrial Product Design. Pages 110–111 present the overview table.

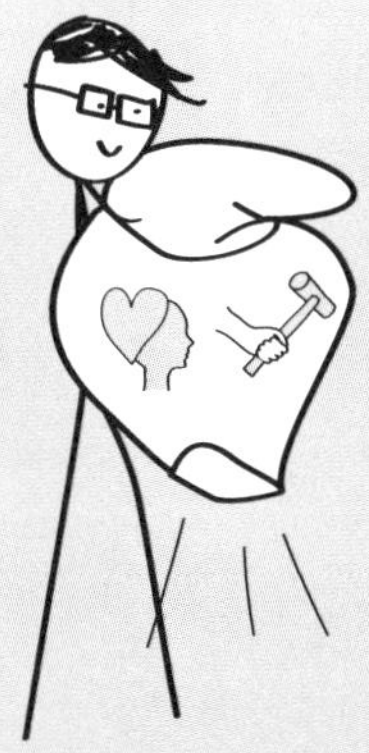

I execute the law.
I value achieving results, especially when they align with my manager's objectives and are clearly reflected in my work.
I believe the market is more efficient than government in delivering public services.
I believe that plans generally work as intended, with only minor, manageable adjustments.
I trust that my manager understands the overarching goal.
I do a good job when I follow procedures, track progress, and deliver as planned.

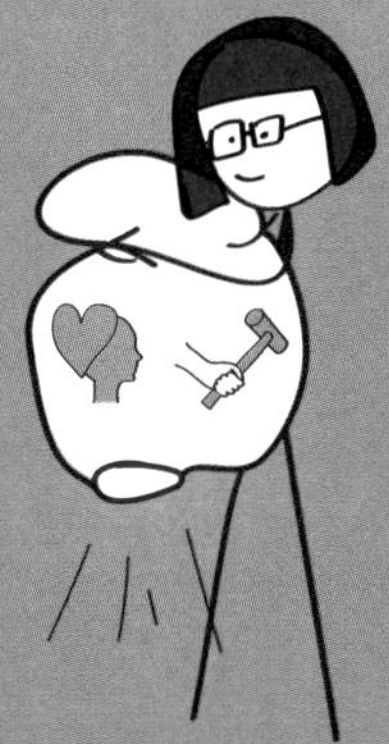

I value creating products that people want to buy and use, product designs I'm proud to call my own. My work contributes to a business.
I believe I need to test my ideas in the real world, because designs rarely work exactly as planned.
There are no fixed procedures in my practice. A good job means delivering a successful product.
The goal is shaped by company needs, technical limits, and what customers are likely to want.

	Traditions in Public Administration	Leading principle in James' context	What is designed	Designed by	
	Stability by Execution <1980		**Practionership of Creation**		
FOUNDATIONS	Change by creation by allround practionership (thinking + doing)	Depends on what is designed	Depends on what is designed	Depends on what is designed	
	Systemworld 1980-2000		**Lifeworld**		
FOCUS	Constitutional + Discretionary	Follow procedures + control execution of public services by the market	Product	Industrial product designer in close relation with experts	
	Collaboration 2000-2020		**Co-Creation**		
	Integration >2020 - Social Designers				

Overview Inherited Baggage

Leading principle in Francis' practice	Designed in the Context of (viability)	Designed for (desirability)	Design realised by (feasibility)
Change by creation by allround practionership (thinking + doing)	Depends on what is designed	Depends on what is designed	Depends on what is designed
New products fulfil needs and bring value to consumers in the Lifeworld	A business	Consumers	Machines (production)

Convergence 2000-2020

With the emergence of digital technologies, there has been a shift to digital products and services in industrial design, creating a new type of designer.
In public administration, the turn of the millennium meant yet another tradition emerging in public administration: the collaborative tradition.
The co-creative element in service design and the need for collaboration in government formed a bridge for designers like Francis to enter the world of James.

'We can design services that do not need a factory for production'

'We need to do it together'

CONVERGENCE

7. Co-Creation

7.1 From Product to Service

Service Design emerged in the early 2000s as a combination of Industrial Product Design Engineering and Marketing, and as a way to 'dematerialise' product design, with the purpose of sustainability. At first glance, the difference between a product and a service seems simple: a product is tangible (you can touch and own it), while a service is intangible (though it might involve physical elements, like a smartphone app). But the real distinction lies deeper. Products are made in factories, usually by machines. Services, on the other hand, are delivered by people within organisations. This changes everything for the designer. The primary material is no longer metal, wood, or plastic; it is people, and increasingly, software.

A service demands human action, turning the designer's **material** from lifeless objects into **people** with emotions and stakes.

Services: levels of tangibility and digitality

With digitalisation, products have developed from three-dimensional to two-dimensional products. The characteristic of the product is less about hardware but more about software. Instead of needing an electrical and mechanical engineer to help the industrial product designer with engineering problems of the product, the digital product designer turns to a software programmer as a technology expert.

In digital products, there may be a connection to a service that requires human action. The Service Designer then frames the digital product (e.g., the app) as a touchpoint of the service. The service itself is a sequence of interrelated actions.

Example of a restaurant:

Imagine you are served in a restaurant. The service has tangible elements, like the food and plates. It has intangible elements, like the way the waiter talks to you or how he moves around in the restaurant. Some restaurants use QR codes to take your order, meaning a digital component enters the service. If a robot were to make your meal and serve your meal, the service would be fully artificial with digital and tangible components, but without human action to execute the service.

From Production to Execution

In industrial product design, production and consumption are separate. A designer does take product and market implementation into account when designing a product—like a stick mixer—which is manufactured, packaged, and sold. The product captures its value independently of the user (see figure 26).

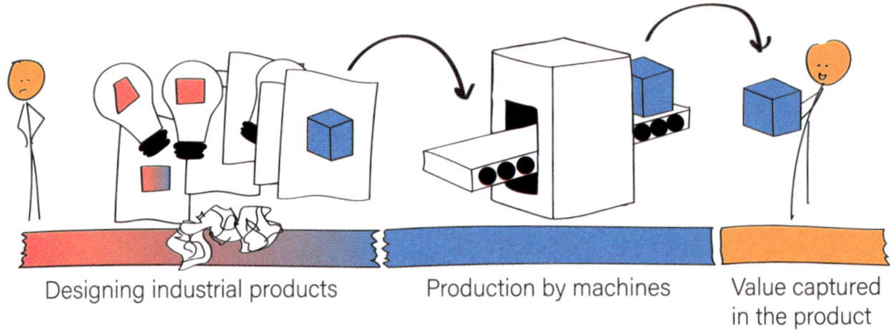

Figure 26: Industrial product design: value captured in the product.

In service design, production and consumption happen simultaneously. The value for the user is created in real time during the execution of the service itself (see figure 27). A service is not a single entity like a product; to capture value, a service is a sequence of interconnected steps. Thus, the value of the service can vary not only because of who is receiving the service, but also by how the service is executed.

Rather than designing a static product, service designers create a system that involves human interactions. That's why the language shifts. What used to be called 'production' becomes 'execution'. And 'implementation', which in industrial product design refers to introducing a completed item to the market, now includes the ongoing act of delivering that service.

Figure 27: Service design: value captured in the execution.

7.2 Consequences for Practitionership

The expansion from designing a product that can be produced to a service that can be executed leads to a new level of complexity. Using the three elements from Industrial Product Design: the desirability of a service, from the consumer or user side, can be treated similarly to that of a product. In terms of business viability, but especially feasibility, service design is different from product design. The designer was educated in the practice of designing industrial products. His practitionership included making decisions to create a plan for an artificial product to be produced in a factory. However, when the design involves people instead of lifeless objects, the practice changes. The 'materials' to work with are now alive and have opinions, emotions, varying levels of expertise, and good and bad days. Essentially, when the designer designs a service that incorporates execution by other humans, the designer is shaping other people's jobs. That has implications.

Firstly, because the design is not a product made by machines but executed by people, designers have to synthesise different types of criteria. Industrial product designers bring together knowledge of materials, mechanics, ergonomics, production processes, and marketing. But service design demands a different set of tools: insights into work organisation, human psychology, group behaviour, and change management in organisations[46]'.

Secondly, the thinking and doing that were an integrated part of the practitionership of designers become untangled because other people execute the design.

> Designing services to be **executed**—not products to be **produced**—fundamentally transforms the designer's role, demanding new knowledge and skills.

CONVERGENCE

Integration to Separation

When a lifeless product gets replaced by humans, the integration of thinking and doing by the designer is challenged. A designer can draw a person instead of a product, no problem[47]. But then, manipulating a material to hold a specific

46 In Anglo-American style, rooted in Taylorism.

47 Generally, product sketches show one person and an object; service sketches show more people and interactions.

form is not the same as manipulating a person to execute a certain task when a new service is to be carried out or a service is redesigned.

If a designer treats the executor the same as material, she would ignore the human side of execution. In fact, she would act as a manager telling an executor what to do because it is how she designed it (see figure 28).

Figure 28: When designers would start telling others what to do...

Paradox of Designing Service Implementation

One of the major challenges designers face after developing a new service is the misconception that scaling it is just a matter of 'rolling it out', similar to how one might scale a product. But scaling the execution of a service is fundamentally different from scaling the production of a product and misunderstanding this can lead to failure in implementation.

When you scale the production of a product, you are increasing output by letting the machines run more or faster. It is a linear

equation when products are produced in mass. If you need more units, you invest in more machines. The product is the same because it is made by the same machines.
Scaling a service is about changing human behaviour and is thus not about repeating a mechanical process. It is scaling human interaction, behaviour, and judgment. Even if designers have co-created a service with a group of practitioners (say, 10 people), scaling[48] requires the other 90 who weren't involved to adopt new ways of working. The new design isn't just about exploring an idea: it is the intention to actually do it, own it, and believe in it.
That is where resistance often appears. Those who were not part of the process may react with confusion or skepticism: 'Why are we doing this? This won't work here.' Their reality hasn't been part of the design nor the design process, so the change feels imposed rather than co-owned.
In hierarchical organisations, it might seem easier: if a decision-maker says, 'We're doing this', then everyone has to follow. But this rarely results in meaningful or sustainable adoption. People may comply, but they don't commit. That created jobs for organisational change managers.
Scaling isn't about replicating the solution exactly. It is about designing how that solution can sustain itself in different settings. That means each new context requires its own attention, adaptation, and design work. Thus, implementing services is not a rollout. It is a redesign, again and again, in

48 When a service is scaled in an organisation is a form of implementation.

each new context.

7.3 The Assembly Line in One Room

'Power' of Employees

Introducing a new service means asking employees to change how they work. And unlike customers, employees can't just walk away; they're expected to adapt (see figure 29).
This creates a unique tension. Employees are on the cost side of the business equation, yet they're also the key to delivering value. Designers assume that if employees don't embrace the change, the service will not be successful because designers are used to looking beyond the behaviour of people, digging for needs. Taking the emotional side of people into account is part of the practice.
Designers will use their analytic, observational, empathic, and creative ways to figure out what the latent needs employees have and why they do what they do.

Figure 29: The power of consumers and the power of employees.

Separation to Integration

Designers understand employees not as obstacles but as collaborators with crucial expertise and insight. Employees are part of the product, part of the 'production', and part of the overall experience for the consumer. But the standardised organisational structure favors separation of tasks and top-down control. Service designers challenge this. They advocate re-integration: bringing different people from the 'assembly line' together as they are all part of making a success of the to-be-designed service. Or bringing together people from different departments that could collaborate on a new service (see figure 30). When they are all in one room, then what?

7.4 Designing with Employees

To design services that actually work out in practice, designers bring 'everyone' involved into the room (from frontline staff to management) because, together, they 'are the service'. It's no longer about designing *for* people, but *with* them.
Designers are used to using tangible materials when they are designing, and they bring their norms and ways of doing with them to the new situation. And so instead of talking and discussing, designers will ask people to use materials to express their thoughts. The creating that they do in tangible materials remains a form of idea generation and a form of understanding the current situation.
This means the designer must get others creative and engaged.

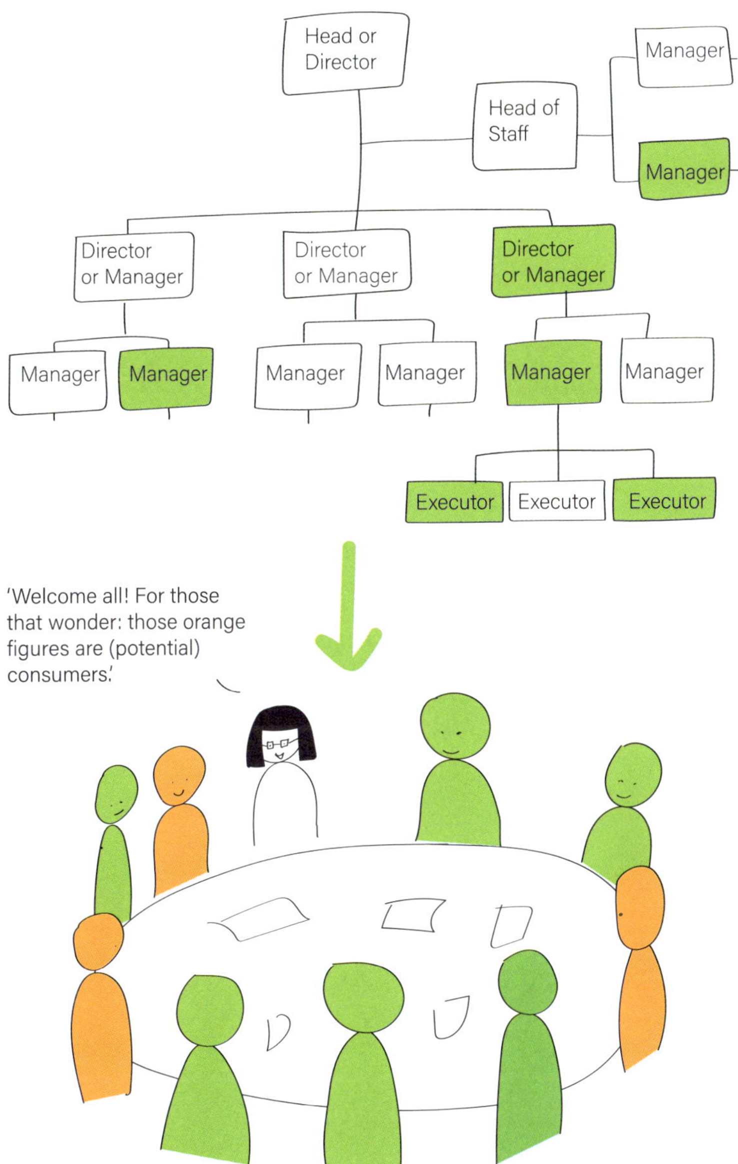

Figure 30: People from all parts of the organisation that can make/ break a new service, including (potential) consumers, at the table.

That requires strong people skills, especially when navigating organisational hierarchies and cultures. Employees are not just shaping a service—they're reshaping their roles. The to-be-designed service will influence their work. In co-creation, participants have the opportunity to create solutions that they would like to have. They can introduce their stakes.

Employees are not just **shaping a service**—they're **reshaping their roles**.

Separating the Stake From the Stakeholder

When designers bring together people with different stakes and ask them to co-create a new service or solution, they may act to protect their own interests. As a result, stakeholders may hold back their true needs and ideas. But designers are precisely looking for these deeper needs because what appears to be conflicting stakes might not actually conflict. This is where design opportunities emerge. If people don't share their genuine perspectives from the start, it becomes difficult for the service designer to recognise these opportunities.

To address this, designers separate the stake from the stakeholder. They do this by materialising the stakes (or perspectives), turning them into visible, shareable artifacts, and laying them out on the table (see figure 31). This helps shift the focus from personal agendas to shared understanding, making room for creative exploration.

Service design differs fundamentally from product design: it deals not with static materials but with people, each with their own roles, emotions, and stakes. Conflicting interests can cause people to hold back. Designers address this by making stakes tangible and shared, shifting the conversation from personal agendas to collective possibilities. This collaborative, stakeholder-centered approach is increasingly relevant, not only in commercial service organisations but also in how governments tackle societal challenges.

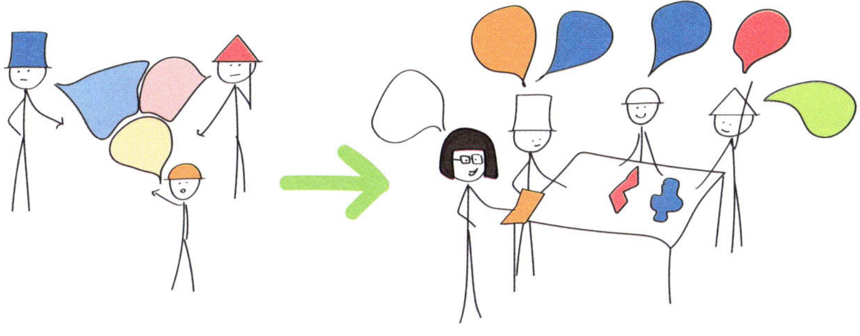

Figure 31: Separating the stake from the stakeholder.

8. Collaboration

8.1 The Collaborative Tradition

In the constitutional tradition, governance was centered around ensuring equality through procedural mechanisms that applied uniformly to all citizens. The discretionary tradition, in contrast, emphasised efficiency by outsourcing services while maintaining government oversight through regulatory controls. In both approaches, governments retained their dominant role as decision-makers and enforcers of public policy. However, as the complexity of societal challenges grew, governments increasingly found themselves in situations where collaboration was not just beneficial but a mere necessity.

The collaborative tradition emerged toward the end of the twentieth century as a response to the increasing complexity brought about by privatisation, digitalisation, globalisation, and the growing recognition of climate change[49]. Governments

49 Braams, et al. (2021).

began to realise that they were no longer fully equipped to address these multifaceted challenges independently. Consequently, they moved beyond relying solely on private sector involvement and started engaging interest groups, branch organisations, and civil society actors in policy design and implementation. This shift was further necessitated by the outsourcing of public services, which resulted in the transfer of specialised knowledge from government institutions to market-based actors[36].
Citizen participation became an essential tool for increasing policy legitimacy (defining if a policy would make sense in the Lifeworld) to increase the feasibility of successful execution. Concepts such as consortia building, public-private collaboration, and quadruple-helix projects (government, private companies, research institutions, and citizens participating together to work on societal challenges) emerged from this new governance paradigm. In this tradition, the government, represented by civil servants, became 'just one of the parties involved' rather than the sole orchestrators of public services (see figure 32).

This shift had two significant consequences.
First, governments relinquished some of their traditional power as the primary providers of public services.
Second, rather than merely overseeing private sector service providers, civil servants actively engaged in partnerships with them, blurring the traditional boundaries between public and private interests. The internal focus on procedures and results

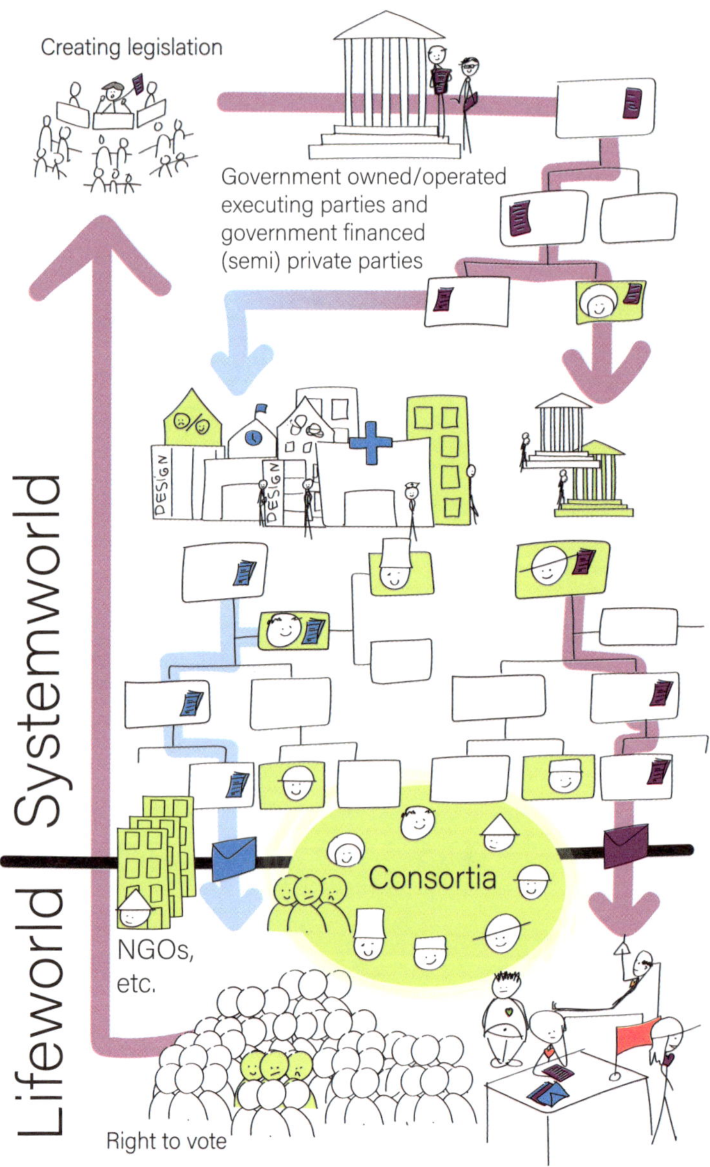

Figure 32: Representation of the collaborative tradition including consortia as example of cross-organisational collaboration.

was complemented by an external focus on collaboration. Civil servants are now asked to follow procedures, create results, and also to step out of the office and take other stakeholders into account to 'solve problems' together with 'the market'. Collaborating with different stakeholders to solve problems sounds a lot like what designers were up to.

8.2 Rise of 'Design Thinking' in Public Administration

In the last two decades of the previous century, ideas from Business Administration were adopted in Public Administration. In the same period, Design Thinking was 'discovered' by Business Administration. It is no wonder that by the turn of the millennium and in the decades that followed, with a need for collaboration, Design Thinking gained popularity in Public Administration. See figure 33 for a quick overview.

Design Thinking in Business Administration[50]

With business administration management as a booming business, it was only a matter of time before design became a focal point in business. Since industrial product designers were educated to give organisations a competitive edge, new

50 Johansson-Sköldberg, et al., (2013).

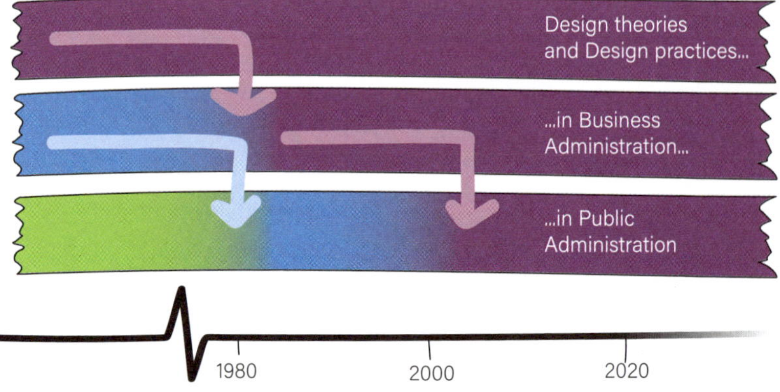

Figure 33: How ideas from design theories and practices entered public administration via business administration.

products were important for survival in business.

Already in the 1970s, designers began speaking the language of business leaders. They reframed design concepts using management terminology, showcasing the value of design through successful case studies.

Their approach was simple: show managers that design wasn't just about how things look, but about how things work, how design could solve problems, improve processes, and ultimately drive business revenues. By doing so, they hoped to make design more accessible and relevant to the decision-makers in organisations.

However, this strategy had an unintended consequence. In their effort to speak a language that managers understood, some of the depth and nuance of design (thinking) was lost. Design Thinking became the equivalent of the practitionership of designers: overly simplified, often painted in broad, optimistic strokes. It was presented as a (business) tool that could solve any problem without fully addressing the complexities and frameworks needed to apply it effectively. While this approach succeeded in generating interest, it sometimes left design (and designers) without the necessary context to be fully understood or implemented in a meaningful way.

Design Thinking as a (workshop) method

While management scholars were invited to explore the world of design, in business practice, design was being brought into the world of management. Design thinking, framed as a 'method[51]', acted as a portal, introducing the business world to design as a strategic tool. Design thinking allowed companies to approach complex problems with a fresh perspective, placing human needs at the center of solutions.
'Design Thinking as a method' created a parallel narrative that existed alongside design theory that educated designers. The parallel narrative resulted in a rise in the popularity of Design Thinking, which also contributed to the rise of social designers. The popularity of Design Thinking also contributed to misunderstandings between designers and non-designers.
Designers do not recognise themselves in these versions of

---

51 These methods are partly derived from Creative Problem Solving methods, making it difficult for non-designers to distinguish Design Thinking from Creative Problem Solving in general.

'Design Thinking'[52].

Design Thinking in Public Administration[53]

The term Design Thinking began appearing in public administration and policy-making literature. It is usually described through a mix of theoretical and practical models. Design Thinking is described as being different from regular thinking because of its focus on desirability—that is, the human side of design. This idea stems from industrial product design rather than design in general. Creativity and exploration are other key elements mentioned to describe Design Thinking, since designing is inherently a creative process with the intention to create 'something new.' Sometimes co-creation is highlighted, which combines human-centredness and creativity.

However, these discussions often leave out two important factors: feasibility (the role of technology) and viability (the business perspective). In some ways, this makes sense. Public administration is not business administration, and in this context, designs are implemented by people rather than machines. But these theoretical descriptions of Design Thinking leave out essential elements that define the practitionership of designers. As the example in the introduction illustrates, boiling potatoes does not define the practice of a chef; neither does co-creation define the practice of a designer.

---

52 Kimbell (2011), and Johansson-Sköldberg, et al., (2013).

53 Hermus, et al., (2020), and van Buuren et al. (2021).

With Design Thinking as a method introduced in businesses and the turn towards collaborative governments and the use of business ideas in public administration, Design Thinking gained traction in governments.
And in a context of civil service where procedures are important, selling the work of a designer as a method makes sense. Because, when designers and the people in their projects step into the world of creating and not knowing the outcome, the structure of a method helps those who are not educated in the design arena. Design Thinking as a method makes designers more relatable for non-designers. At least there is a method to hold on to.

Design Thinking in Design Theory

In the 1980s, books on design methods and journals on design emerged and consolidated design as a scientific discipline. In the same period, a new wave of design research emerged from the popularity of cognitive psychology: if we understand how designers think, we can design better. In design theory, the term Design Cognition is used to discuss this. Terminology around Design Cognition includes a 'Designerly way of Knowing'[54], from Nigel Cross, referring to the creative, iterative nature of designing. Also, 'Reflection-in-Action', as discussed in the Foundations and Abductive Reasoning—which I'll get to in the next part—are terms used to discuss Design Cognition.

54 Cross (2006).

9. Rise of the Social Designer

9.1 Together We Can

With the collaborative focus in Service Design, the collaborative tradition emerging in Public Administration, Design Thinking functioned as a bridge between designers and civil servants. Norms and values converged to a collaborative thinking and mindset of 'yes, we need to change to handle societal challenges.' This convergence paved the way for the rise of the social designer. Designers who combine their design practitionership with a deep commitment to societal change through collaboration.

The Bridge That Misleads

Design Thinking methods ignore the practitionership that is needed to use these methods well. In terms of Schön's Reflection-in-Action: Design Thinking methods are 'knowing how' instead of 'knowing that'.

Design Thinking methods ignore the experiences of designers immersing in a context to get a feel for their potential clients, so they 'know' what to design. They neglect the skills needed to communicate ideas through a drawing or 3D model. Design Thinking methods overlook the delicate ways of finding ways to test ideas with potential clients in the Lifeworld to move forward with concepts, neglecting to mention the painful experience of 'darlings that need to be killed' and the trade-offs that need to be made because the organisation only has a machine to create squared shapes, not round ones.

Design Thinking is celebrated for its focus on the Lifeworld: we need to create better services for citizens, and designers (educated in the legacy of industrial product design) made a living by focusing on needs in the Lifeworld. It makes sense that the focus on the Systemworld ignored the reality of citizens.

However, the 'empathising with the user' part does not do justice to designing; it ignores the criteria designers take into account regarding the factors of feasibility and viability. 'Will our design bring value to the organisation?' and 'Can we produce the design?' Or, in service design: 'Can we execute the design?' With the note that an employee has a different agency than a consumer.

When designers moved toward designing in the public domain, new questions arise. Like an employee, but different, a citizen has a different agency than a consumer. And moreover, a public administration is not like a business.

9.2 Inherited Baggage Convergence

Page 137 summarises the inherited baggage from the focus on the discretionary tradition and the discipline of Industrial Product Design. Pages 138–139 present the overview table.

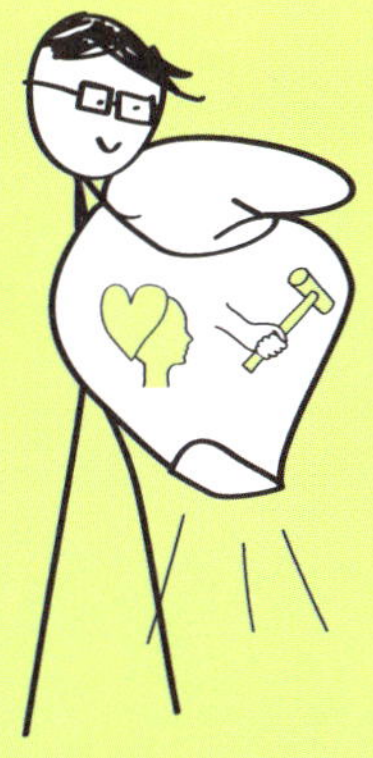

I execute the law.

I value equal treatment. I value collaboration to work on societal issues.

I believe we need to collaborate to address societal issues.

I believe that we need all stakeholders at the table for collaboration. I do a good job of getting all parties involved to work on a societal issue.

I value new services that bring value to people.

I believe when employees are part of executing a service, they should be part of designing the service.

I believe that creating together is the way to achieve a good service.

I do a good job when I am part of creating new services, together with the people who have influence on and are influenced by the service.

	Traditions in Public Administration	Leading principle in James' context	What is designed	Designed by
FOUNDATIONS	**Stability by Execution <1980**		**Practionership of Creation**	
	Constitutional (bureaucracy)	Follow procecedures to execute the law	Everything artifical: created by humans	Designer
FOCUS	**Systemworld 1980-2000**		**Lifeworld**	
	Constitutional + Discretionary	Follow procedures + control execution of public services by the market	Product	Industrial product designer in close relation with experts
CONVERGENCE	**Collaboration 2000-2020**		**Co-Creation**	
	Constitutional + Discretionary + Collaborative	Follow procedures + control execution + we need to collaborate with parties	Service	Service designer in co-creation with the people that can make/break the service
	Integration >2020 - Social Designers			

Overview Inherited Baggage

	Leading principle in Francis' practice	Designed in the Context of (viability)	Designed for (desirability)	Design realised by (feasibility)
	Change by creation by allround practionership (thinking + doing)	Depends on what is designed	Depends on what is designed	Depends on what is designed
	New products fulfil needs and bring value to consumers in the Lifeworld	A business	Consumers	Machines (production)ww
	Creating together to ensure that people can bring value to consumers	A business	Consumers	Employees perhaps with people from other parties and users (execution)

Dynamic Quo

>2020

DYNAMIC QUO

The worlds of Francis and James are coming together. But wait: a citizen has a different type of power than a consumer, and a public administration is not like a business.
There are job positions in James' department that Francis could fill, based on a design focus on desirability, feasibility and viability. And in her work, Francis integrates 4 types of reasoning, 5 perspectives, 5 dimensions and 3 goals.
Yet one big question still lingers – the elephant in the room: What exactly does Francis design?

10. Integration

10.1 The Transformative Tradition

With the bureaucratic, discretionary system still in place, it meant more and more planning and control systems were developed to help civil servants 'stay in control'. Automation and computer technology made it possible to build systems that filled that need. It turned out that we are in a situation in which we have lost flexibility due to the systems we have built. With computer technology moving faster than ever, tension grows between the computer systems that are out there and the computer systems (and following ways of organising) that exist in governments.

In 1973, Rittel & Webber made an argument that the rational, predictable approach to dealing with societal issues is failing. In the decades that followed, this approach remained dominant and became increasingly rigid based on the institutionalisation of privatised organisations as well as dependencies on computer systems. Societal challenges lingering for decades, like climate change and the steady growth of the world population, require entire societies to transition to a new direction. Governments have a directive role to play in these societal transitions[1].

In bureaucratic, market, and collaborative traditions, it remains difficult for governments to take the necessary role needed to make transitions for climate change and move beyond neoliberal societies. Governments are not fit to take the lead that is required to make these transitions happen.

a new tradition is in the making (and needed) to fulfill the governmental tasks in transitions.

In transformative governments[55], civil servants are holistic, future-minded, abductive thinkers[56]. Designers seem to hold the mindsets and skills fitting in transformative governments, at least for now.

Arriving in the Moment

Francis takes all her implicit values, beliefs, norms and behaviours along in her backpack, then she steps into the world James is familiar with. At first glance, designing a product for a business and designing within the civil service of a government might seem like parallel processes. They both require planning, iteration, and execution. When we look closer, the norms and values stemming from the legacies of governing and designing cause friction. The system in public administration seeks to preserve what designers seeks to

---

55 Braams et al. (2021).

56 Abduction is a form of reasoning, explained in chapter 11.

transform. Where one sees the value of equality in procedures, the other sees constraint to creativity. One believes in the power of planning, the other in the necessity of adapting. One measures what was delivered; the other values how it was shaped and the value it brings. Public administration brings order, accountability, and fairness; designers bring creativity, adaptability, and responsiveness.
When product designers started to explore designing services something happened for the feasibility aspect of designing. When designers move from a business to a public organisation, 'business viability' becomes 'public organisation viability', or in case of Francis and James 'public administration viability'. Moreover, the role of the receiver of the realised designs changes from a consumer to a citizen, changing the meaning of desirability.

10.2 Consumer Power vs. Citizen Power

The step between commercial service designer and social service designer seems small. Yet the receiving side of the design, so the consumer or the citizen have a different type of power.

Follow the Money

The role of money in government is fundamentally different

from its role in business. In a business, money is spent with the primary goal of earning more money than money spent. Ultimately, decision-making revolves around whether an investment will generate more revenue than it costs, which is essential for the survival of the company. In a government, survival is generally less of a concern—at least in Western democracies over the last eighty years. The role of money is to serve the public and (or) reach political goals.

Consumer, Buyer, User, Citizen

In a commercial setting, the consumer holds power to (not) to buy. If dissatisfied with a product or service, they can simply spend their money elsewhere. This dynamic creates an incentive for businesses to continuously refine their offerings to remain competitive. It also creates an incentive for industrial product and service designers to involve potential buyers in their design processes: they do better design something that enough people want to buy.

Consumers, traditionally[57], take two types of roles: the user or the buyer. Take for example diapers. The parent buys the diapers. The baby is the main user of the diaper, but the parent is also a user of the diaper because the parent changes the diaper. In this example the main user has little power of choice. But if the baby gets a diaper rash the buyer may switch

57 I say 'traditionally' because the division between buyer and seller started to blur, because of social media and new business models in which buyers become sellers.

to another brand. The buyer has the power of choice but the satisfaction of the user with the product does influence the buyers behaviour.

Citizens, however, do not have the same agency. Public services are often the only option available. If they are inadequate, a citizen cannot simply 'switch providers' without leaving their country, a decision far more complex than choosing a different phone brand. Public services lack consumer sovereignty, meaning citizens cannot reject a service in the same way a customer rejects a bad product[58].

Citizens are 'users' of products and services provided by the government. But citizens are not are not the direct buyers of these products and services. They pay taxes and through a system of governing they receive products and services on the other end.

Consumers engage in a direct transactional relationship with

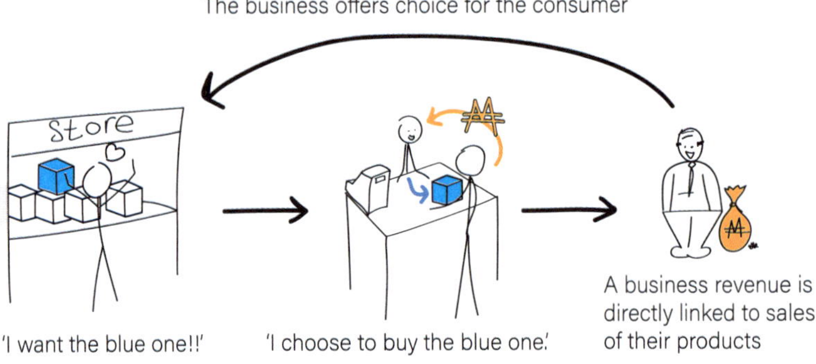

Figure 34: Direct value transaction between consumer and a business.

58 Osborn & Browne (2011).

businesses (see figure 34).
You buy and you receive what you buy. Citizens have a more passive role as 'users' of government services. Citizens pay taxes and they vote.
In case a citizen needs a public service, he applies for the service, but may not have to pay for that service. The closest citizens come to a 'buying' position is during elections, and even then, their influence is diluted compared to the direct power of a consumer's purchasing choice. Their value transaction is indirect (see figure 35). There is no direct link feedback loop between the policy or service that is offered and the acceptance of the public.

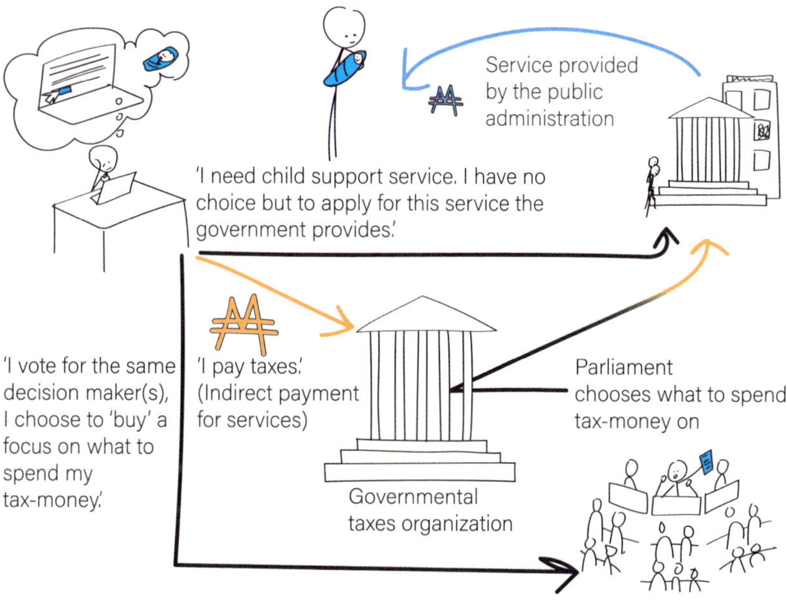

Figure 35: Indirect value transaction between citizen and a government.

As a consequence, involving citizens in designing public services or policies is less obvious then for a product or service designer.

Example of The National Archive

The National Archive in the Netherlands is a government owned executing organisation under the Ministry of Education, Culture and Science. The task of the National Archive is to make historic documents accessible. As a citizen, if you want to look up historic documentation you need to make an appointment online and the archive is open on working days. From the perspective of the task of the National Archive you could say: yes, the documents are made accessible. From the perspective of a citizen that works five days a week and is not good with computers, the archive is not quite accessible.
But, following the task of the National Archive, they are executing their task, at least from a system's perspective. An employee might not feel the urge to create a change in the procedure. Work is already busy enough.

10.3 Business Administration vs. Public Administration

Definition of Success

Traditionally, businesses operate on financial incentives

(Return on Investments). Success is measured in profits, sales, and market share. Value added for the consumer leads to value (money) for the business. These days, businesses also include different measures of success, such as self-inclined sustainability goals, for example. In the end, a business can only survive when it makes a profit.

Defining success for a product or service is more complex in a government than in business products and services.

Success in the implementation of a policy is measured in four different categories[59]. Firstly, the question of whether the policy reached its intended goals; secondly, whether the process was effective and efficient; thirdly, whether the political conditions necessary for policy success are met, and how the associated costs and benefits are distributed among the (political) actors involved; and fourthly, the endurance assessment: the three elements above should not be assessed once but over a period of time and in different contexts.

Definition of Failure

Measuring the intended goals of the product and expected revenue is also a business measure to indicate success. A business may also measure the effectiveness and efficiency of the process of designing the product. But the third element to measure the success of a policy, the political success, creates a different dynamic in the context of James in relation to that of Francis's traditional context.

---

59 Compton & Hart (2019).

When a product is not successful and it does not bring in the money as was assumed, the business can choose to cut the product. In some organisations, the business owner(s) may fire the decision maker for the go/no-go on the product, the person who, according to the organisational hierarchy, is responsible. The business owner may lose money, but he remains in the same position.
That is different in politics. The politician responsible for a specific policy may lose position when his policy fails, by not getting re-elected, or if worse, he needs to stand down during his term. For politicians, it may be better not to measure the results of an implemented policy. It may not live up to the promise the politician made, costing votes. On the other hand, if policies are not evaluated, it is difficult to learn from the choices that were made.

10.4 Consequences for Practitionership

Practitionership changes because citizens have a different agency than consumers. Practitionership changes because business success is different from success in politics. And success in politics influences public administration.

Practitionership in Public Organisations

Designing within public-private service organisations—such

as hospitals, schools, or eldercare facilities—comes with a unique paradox. The professionals who deliver these services, like doctors, teachers, or caregivers, are highly trained experts. Yet, in practice, they are often treated as mere implementers of decisions made by managers or policy-makers.

Take healthcare as an example. General practitioners undergo extensive training, yet they often work in tightly controlled systems where their input into how care is organised is limited. Managers and administrators create the frameworks within which they must operate, often without fully involving them in the design process.

Designers who step into these environments notice this tension. They are expected to design systems or services in which the practitioners—doctors, in this case—seem to be both users and providers. This creates a conceptual confusion: is the doctor the user of the system, the provider of the service, or even the 'product' delivering value to the patient?

From a designer's perspective, this is problematic. Designers see people not as tools or products, but as active, thinking individuals. They also respect the expertise of professionals. Designers are not medical experts, and they don't pretend to know how to treat patients. In a context where the executor of their ideas is a practitioner, the question is: why not have the practitioner design his/her own work?

Designers can find themselves in a strange position—shaping the organisation of care, even though they are not practitioners themselves. This risks turning designers into the thinkers, while the actual practitioners remain executors.

Designers use their skills to empower practitioners. Instead of designing systems that constrain professional judgment, designers can create environments that support it—where practitioners have space to practice their expertise fully. In this way, designers can help bridge the gap between management thinking and professional doing.

'Francis, James, you have been silent for a while. Are you still with us?'
'Yes, I'm thinking', answers Francis.
'Me too. I'm thinking about what that means for me. I guess I recognise these three traditions in public administration, also in my colleagues. Some are fans of the first, others of the second, and most I work with are fans of the third. This 'transformative tradition' seems like a nice way to go. I also see the value of separating stakes from the stakeholders, as you call it. I don't know; I'm wondering what type of job I would then give to Francis', contemplates James.
'So, yeah, turns out I've got a bit of a blind spot when it comes to designing for public administration', begins Francis. 'Or, honestly, any public organisation. I have encountered the 'conceptual confusion', as you call it. When we designed a new vision for collaboration in diabetes care for children, paediatricians were involved (see figure 36). Since we were designing the collaboration itself, all stakeholders were, in a way, users of that collaboration. But the real aim was better care

for diabetic children—so ultimately, the children and their parents were the true users of what we designed. The professionals, like doctors, weren't users of the collaboration; they were the collaboration', Francis thinks aloud.

'Or you could say they're executing the collaboration. With your help, they were designing what they're supposed to execute. But because the Diabetic Care Foundation paid you to design this vision, they may feel they hold decision-making power. The other stakeholders you invited might feel less ownership of the outcome. They care about the children, but they have

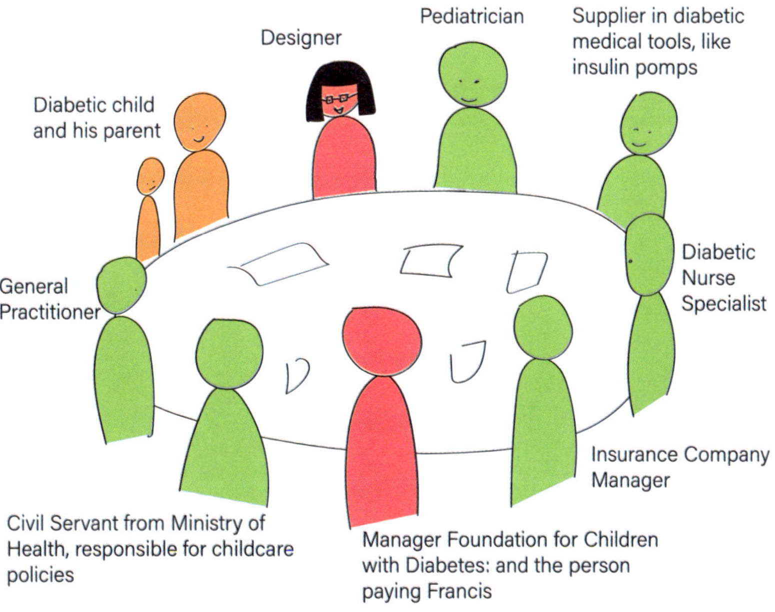

Figure 36: Francis and the stakeholders she got in one room.

different stakes. They're not the users or executors in the organisation—they belong to different organisations. What you were probably aiming for was a shared goal that could unite them. But one session doesn't create shared responsibility. People go home and return to their usual routines. That's why you need to repeat the process, over and over—you need endurance.
Great job getting everyone in the room, by the way; that must have been a challenge.'
'To say the least. Sometimes I feel more like an event organiser than a designer.'
'I guess you are.'
'Hm, that doesn't feel right. It's part of my practitionership but doesn't define my practitionership, as you put it. I still struggle to 'sell myself' to people like Roy, even though James might be starting to get what I'm about. Like he said himself—what is my job, exactly?'
'Your job exactly depends on you and your context. Generally, I see three job positions for you, Francis. In these roles, you can enrich and add layers of understanding and action to public administration, helping you achieve the impact you want. I'll discuss them in the next chapter.'

11. Social Designers

11.1 Three Positions for Social Designers

Status quo

Today, designers can mostly be found[60] in local governments, like municipalities, or in executing organisations working on public services. In policy labs, they often involve multiple stakeholders to create future visions and scenarios for specific complex societal issues. In the first position, the government misses the value of designers' ability to pinpoint the 'right' problem to address because the solution is already defined as well as the problem beforehand.

In the second position, governments miss the value of designers' ability to attach future scenarios (desirability and viability) to daily operations (feasibility aspect) because they lack the authority to bring these scenarios further in the

60 Hermus et al. (2020).

government[61]. The value that is missed here is the designers' integrative approach.

Integrated and Focused

Force-fitting the factors of viability, desirability, and feasibility into designing in public administration, three types of function titles emerge:

- Social- or Public Service Designer, with a focus on desirability.
- Policy Designer, with a focus on viability.
- Organisational Designer, with a focus on feasibility.

See figure 37 for an overview of the positions of these three function titles of social designers.

'Francis, remember you said you integrate perspectives during your job interview?'
'Yes, don't remind me', Francis says.
'Integrating perspectives can be interpreted as 'getting stakeholders on board', which is also true, but something that James already does, right?'
'Well, yes. We often have sessions with corporations and other stakeholders to discuss policies', James concurs.
'I take other stakeholders into account?' doubts Francis.
'Yes, but why and which ones? Perhaps we can say that James is integrating perspectives from different parties on a policy level, so all the different stakeholders focus

61 Lewis et al. (2020), and Clarke & Craft (2019).

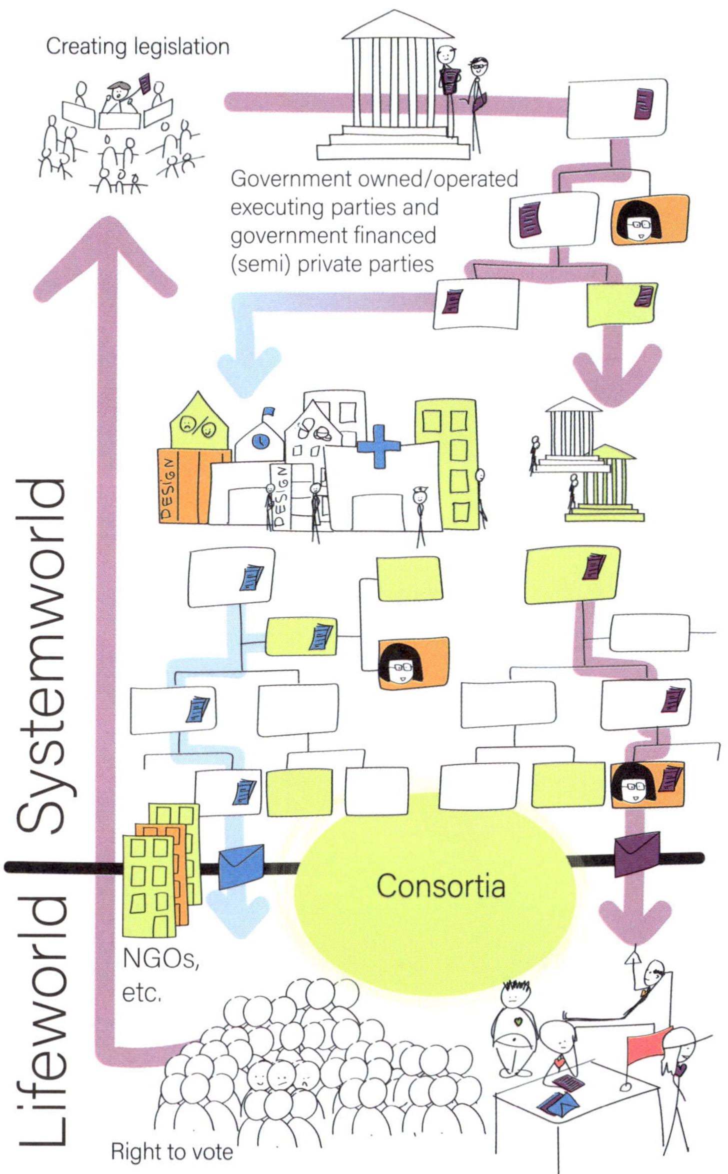

Fig 37. Overview like figure 12, 25 and 32. In this figure extra attention to three positions for designers. In each position a different focus.

on viability: what is in it for our organisation. Thereby, they miss out on asking the other questions.'
'But some of the stakeholders are also executing our policies', James argues.
'Do the people you invite execute your policies, or do they then tell other people what to do?'
'Both, I guess. But I mean, you cannot get all these people together. I'm already happy when one person from an organisation shows up', answers James.
'What about the people that have to actually execute these policies? And what about the people who are influenced by the execution of these policies, you know, citizens?' Francis asks.
'Exactly.'

No matter what functional position a designer holds in the organisational chart, the focus on either desirability, viability, or feasibility does mean an exclusion of the other two factors. For example, when their focus is on policies (viability), it doesn't mean they forget what people should benefit from the policy, what the impact could be for citizens in the Lifeworld (desirability), and not to forget who is going to execute this policy (feasibility). That is why Francis integrates perspectives from different types of stakeholders.
Some might say that designers take a holistic approach. Organisational Designers, focusing on the internal procedures and processes (execution, thus feasibility), will consider the purpose of a process and do not see 'the way we do things' as

separate from what it should achieve in terms of executing the law (viability) and providing for citizens (desirability). A policy designer, far removed from citizens on the organisational chart, still seeks to understand what citizens find desirable. Likewise, a Public Service Designer can feel frustrated by decisions made higher up in the hierarchy, where considerations of desirability and feasibility may have been overlooked in their eyes.

When Roy the Recruiter was confused about Francis and whether she was an Organisational Change Agent, it was because of her focus on execution as well as her consideration of whether it is worthy for the organisation and for the final receiver. Coming from the legacies of Industrial Product Design, Francis, in her role as Organisational Designer, adopts a different approach than a traditional organisational change agent, who was trained under the presumption of the separation of tasks.

Moreover, Francis uses two types of reasoning beyond deductive and inductive reasoning, and she won't limit herself to only talking with stakeholders. Francis works in five dimensions. And Francis has five perspectives on reality.

'I do?' asks Francis.

'Yes, you do. You could even argue that you work in sixty dimensions, or sixty ways of doing.'

'Sixty?!' she exclaims.

'Yes, you'll see what I mean.'

11.2 Two Types of Reasoning

To move forward in unknown situations, designers use two types of reasoning. A few years ago, a politician in the Netherlands suggested that a law should be created that obligated primary schools only to use scientifically approved teaching methods[62]. He based his idea on research that showcased that schools are using many unscientific methods. In the Netherlands, the 'quality of the results of kids' in school is decreasing. He sees this as a solution to that problem.

'I remember this!' Francis interrupts. 'When I read this, I thought: why? Why is this the answer? What about the fact that there are not enough teachers, and that the administrative load is high? My initial thought was that this idea would only lead to more problems.' Francis starts to get wound up.

'Why so agitated? The idea didn't make it', tries James.

'You could say that the politician reasons through 'explanatory abduction.'

'Through what?' they say in chorus.

'Explanatory abduction. We can distinguish four types of reasoning: Induction, Deduction, Explanatory Abduction, and Creative or Innovative Abduction[63]. You use explanatory abduction in your work too, Francis.'

62 Van Soest (2021).

63 Roozenburg & Eekels (1995), and Dorst (2011).

Quick reminder of Deduction and Induction

In deductive reasoning, we move from the general to the specific. A well-known example is:

- General statement: All humans are mortal.
- Specific case: Socrates is a human.
- Conclusion: Socrates is mortal.

This reasoning seeks truth. However, the initial statements (premises) must be true; otherwise, the conclusion is unlikely to be true—though not impossible.

In inductive reasoning, we draw general conclusions from specific cases. This is the method used in empirical science. For example:

- Observation 1: If glass is heated, it expands.
- Observation 2: If copper is heated, it expands.
- Observation 3: If steel is heated, it expands.
- General conclusion: If any material is heated, it expands.

This isn't definitive like Socratic logic. Inductive reasoning is less truth-bound than deduction, yet it's how we uncover knowledge. It often works because the reasoning is sound. In the example: most materials expand when heated (though water below 4°C does not). So, the conclusion may not be held for every material, but it fits many. We investigate where it applies and where it doesn't, gradually approaching 'the truth'. This is the essence of empirical research.

Explanatory Abduction

Explanatory abduction is a form of reasoning that moves from an observed effect (a symptom, outcome, or phenomenon) to a possible underlying cause. It follows the logic of: 'If this effect occurs, what might explain it?' Rather than providing deductive certainty, abduction offers the best possible explanation based on available evidence.

It follows this general pattern:

- Observation (Consequence): Something has happened or is the case.
- Rule (General Statement): If a certain cause were true, it would explain the observation.
- Hypothesis (Antecedent): Therefore, the cause might be true.

This is reasoning backwards from consequence to cause. To use your example, Francis:

- Observation (Consequence): Schoolkids do poorly in school.
- General Rule (Premise 1): If unscientific teaching methods are used, kids' school performances are decreasing.
- Hypothesised Cause (Premise 2): Unscientific teaching methods are being used.
- Conclusion: The poor results of kids are likely due to the use of unscientific methods.

This is an explanatory abduction: we see a problem (kids' school performances are decreasing), we know one plausible explanation (use of unscientific teaching methods), and we infer the cause. However, this type of reasoning is not logically certain. The same observed problem (kids' low school performance) could have other causes: teacher burnout, classroom size, poor infrastructure, or socio-economic factors. That's why abductive reasoning is always tentative and open to revision as more information becomes available. Its conclusions need to be tested or supported with further evidence because it deals in plausibility, not proof.

In the political arena, if you say it often enough, it becomes proof.

Creative Abduction

Where explanatory abduction seeks to explain existing phenomena, creative abduction refers to a more generative form of abductive reasoning. It involves imagining new possibilities: potential futures, solutions, or systems that could fulfill the desired effect or solve a problem.

Creative abduction is not about identifying what is but about proposing what could be. It is the main type of reasoning designers use, bridging a gap between current reality and desired outcomes.

- Desirable Outcome (Goal): What do we want to achieve?
- Possible Conditions (Creative Hypothesis): What could make that outcome possible?
- Proposed Intervention: Let's create or test a new approach to achieve it.

In the example of introducing scientifically based teaching methods:

- Goal: Children should learn to read and write better.
- Hypothesis: If we implement a law requiring the use of scientifically validated teaching methods, outcomes will improve.
- Proposed Intervention: Let's design a policy mandating

evidence-based methods in schools.

In this case, Francis disagrees with the hypothesis because she believes other possible conditions are at work. Unlike explanatory abduction, creative abduction moves from what should happen to what could bring it about. If a designer is asked to execute a proposed intervention or a hypothesis as fact, they question if the hypothesis is true.

Designers have internalised both ways of abductive reasoning. Industrial Product Designers and Service Designers make their living by digging up consumers' latent needs (explanatory abduction) and creating a solution for those needs (creative abduction). Therefore, designers focus on details to figure out the assumptions that are overlooked, to create space to design. And in design, the first criteria for any idea popping up is: will it adhere to the needs? Will the idea actually solve the problem of the consumer?

Whenever designers are given a solution to further develop or execute, their initial response is: why? What values does this solution bring? Designers' initial focus will be on understanding why things are as they are and figuring out the (hidden) relationships in the situation, and then creating a more desired outcome.

11.3 Sixty Ways of Doing

Zero and One Dimension

Civil servants use words on paper. Written text is linear; it goes in one direction and is therefore one-dimensional. Politicians use spoken words. Spoken words have zero dimensions; they disappear in thin air. Public administration is a world built on words. Law is written, after all. Legal texts are crafted to reduce ambiguity as much as possible. For judges, lawyers, and civil servants, clarity and singular interpretation are essential. But language operates on a highly abstract level; it is one of the most cognitively demanding forms of communication. It is also the superior way of communicating in our societies.
Designers also speak (duh) and write. But they use three more dimensions for two reasons: to think and to communicate.

The Second Dimension: Visuals

When it comes to change and creation, especially when trying to describe situations that do not yet exist, language may fall short. Words are abstract, and when used to imagine hypothetical or future situations, which are themselves abstract, they can obscure more than they reveal. Using language when trying to make sense of a big topic like climate change, ideas remain abstract, clouded in our heads.
This is where images can help. Visuals are, in a sense, closer to nature; they depict reality more directly than language does. While it is true that pictures can have multiple interpretations, they can also provide clarity that words often cannot. The word

'imagination' itself contains the root 'image', reminding us of the power of visual thinking.

Images, drawings, and sketches are often viewed as inferior, perhaps because they are more instinctive; children can draw long before they can read or write.

In a context like public administration, where precision in language is critical and rationality is an important value as a means for equal treatment, the openness of visual communication can feel risky, suspicious, even childish, and therefore not taken seriously.

One might argue that abstract language suits abstract thought. But in practice, this often leads to endless discussion without shared understanding. Visual representations can cut through abstraction, offering a shared reference point. Paradoxically, while visuals may invite multiple interpretations, they can also create more immediate clarity, especially when exploring something that does not yet exist.

3D and 4D

Visuals may draw us nearer to nature, yet they remain but images for the eye. A deeper, more embodied experience arises when thought and communication extend into three dimensions—where the mind's work takes shape, and you can truly feel its contours. Here, famous building blocks from a Danish company come into play, alongside clay and humble scraps of material, as ideas are given form.

And then comes the fourth dimension: time. In this realm, thought and dialogue take flight as a pilot, some might call the test. Yet, in truth, all the dimensions that came before were their own tests as well—steps in an ongoing dance of designing change.

'That is true. In my context, drawings are viewed as childish. Using LEGO® bricks, however, is accepted in my department, since we conducted a workshop where LEGO played a central role', reflects James.
'I've definitely seen those faces of resistance', Francis replies. 'Whenever I bring out white paper and markers, people hesitate at first. They always end up enjoying it, but they're reluctant to get started.'
'It's not childish at all. When you work in different dimensions, beyond just spoken or written words, you activate different parts of the brain.'
'I use drawing as a way to think too', Francis adds thoughtfully.

Use Dimension, By Whom, About What

Traditionally, product designers have used sketches in two main ways:
As a tool for thinking: not necessarily to communicate with others, but to generate and explore new ideas for themselves.
And as a means of communication: to convey product ideas to others. Drawings help express the functionality, aesthetics, and overall concept of an idea, or a combination of these elements, making it easier for others to understand and engage with the design.

Not only sketching but also speaking, writing, 3D prototypes, and even playing out a sequence of actions (4D) can be used to communicate and think.
In service design, where value is created through a sequence of actions rather than a static product, and where co-creation plays a key role, visualisation takes on an even broader function. Designers encourage others to visualise—not just to communicate, but also to think. Visual tools like images, sketches, drawings, or even cartoons help people shift their perspective, enabling them to understand the current situation more clearly, envision a desired future, and identify the first steps toward change. Even more so for 3D and 4D tools.
The more interdependencies there are, the more complex the situation becomes. In these cases, visualisation is not only used to imagine what could be but also to make sense of what currently exists. It helps bring clarity to complexity.
The final variable is what to focus on: either on the current situation, the desired situation, or ideas for moving toward the desired situation.
That leaves us with five dimensions: for thinking and communication about the situation, for yourself as a designer and to have others do that, about the situation, the desired situation, and (or) about ideas for making moves, which equals 5 times 2 times 2 times 3, resulting in sixty ways as a combination of 'used dimension', 'by whom', and 'about what' (see figure 38).

Figure 38: Sixty ways of doing: used dimension, by whom, about what.

11.4 Five Perspectives on Reality

Another way to describe the ways of working of social designers is by using the Viability, Desirability, and Feasibility perspectives to focus on different layers that are at work simultaneously and also interact with each other. Designers incorporate five layers in their work. For them, each of these perspectives is real (see figure 39).

- Head: The rational layer: how a process is supposed to function, step by step.
- Hands: The practical layer: what happens in daily reality.
- Heart: The emotional layer: how people feel within the system.
- Lifeless elements: The physical or digital tools and structures involved.
- Whole: The systemic layer: the interdependence and dynamics between all of the above-mentioned layers.

Figure 39: Five perspectives on reality.

Head

The Head represents rationality and objectivity. The Head is the main reality in public administration. It is represented by the value of 'highly' (meaning in theory) educated people and the use of language as the most abstract form of communication.

An example of how the Head exposes itself is through a flowchart. A flowchart shows how a process is supposed to work. Flowcharts assume order and clarity. They reflect theoretical structure (the Head). The flowchart does not focus on how the flow is executed in reality (the Hands) or how people experience it in both providing and receiving roles (the Heart). They are language-based and often ambiguous, lacking connection to real practice or emotion. Even when a flowchart is made out of icon pictures, if it does not enrich what we know with our Heads, it fails to provide new information. For example, when the chart says, 'push a button' and we see someone pushing a button, it doesn't give new information.

Hands

Hands are a metaphor for how ideas take shape in the real world, whether through the hands of citizens who receive or those of public servants who implement the law. This human layer was long overlooked in public administration, but interest is growing in testing new policies through small-scale pilots.

For designers rooted in the tradition of industrial product design, hands symbolise the connection to the tangible. They are where thought meets touch, where ideas become real. In the hands, all senses come alive—making human experience not just visible, but a bodily experience that can be deeply felt. This is a nice lead-up to the next layer.

Heart

Designers focus on the heart. Desire and motivation start there. In academic or rational settings like public administration, facts are seen as the only objective truth. But designers recognise another kind of truth: emotional truth. If people feel something is unfair, confusing, or frustrating, that feeling is real, no matter what the data says.

Designers don't see emotion as the opposite of reason. They treat feelings as valid data. It is evidence of how a system is experienced. Instead of correcting perceptions with facts, they use those experiences as design goals, shaping solutions that respond to both logic and emotion.

Lifeless Elements

Designers always consider lifeless elements—they are the foundation of design. Designing is a human act, rooted in the science of artificial things. Though technology has shifted from mechanical to electronic and from 3D to 2D, these elements remain lifeless.

Public administration also deals with lifeless elements. Digital services offer real-time, personalised options and potential cost savings. However, the tools used in these systems are deeply embedded in how work is done. Changing software means training staff and transferring data, which is costly and complicated.

The Whole

Because designers need to synthesise a solution using criteria that have different types of sources, they look at situations from a whole perspective because these sources are interconnected and dependent on each other. The whole is the legacy of all-around practitioners of design.
In public administration, which is organised through task division, taking the whole perspective is not easy. You can also see what is nearby, not on the other side of the organisational chart. In the collaborative tradition in public administration, the whole perspective has started to get more attention.

'How are you doing Francis?'
'I wonder how to use less words than you did to explain my value in the context of public administration and for my friends also about other public organisations', answers Francis.
'What about the elephant in the room?'
'What elephant?'
'The question that defined your practitionership: what do you design?'
'Oh that, hm.'

11.5 The Elephant in the Room

Final Overview

The final overview of inherited baggage, following the chronology of four traditions in public administration, is at the end of this chapter (pages 178-179). In a public administration shaped by these four traditions, social designers can help create positive change. Their practice, rooted in the legacy of industrial design, must adapt to work with or within public administration or public organisations. One question remains: what does a social designer actually design?

Universalisation

Design scholars presume universality among design disciplines in their study of design. In the past decades, another type of universalisation took place. Not the universalisation of human creation, but that of the universalising act of designing emerged from the legacy of the design discipline of industrial product design. The 77 labels of design[64] do not include labels from design fields like architecture, mechanical engineering, art, urban planning, or policy design. All labels are founded in the legacy of industrial product design.

Perhaps, ultimately, any form of design is a form of creation and therefore involves changing the way things are. That does create a situation that describes designing so abstractly that it includes everything, like the idea of going to the beach, which

64 Stappers, Sleeswijk Visser, & van Boeijen (2023).

James mentioned at the beginning. The universalisation of industrial product design imposes the question on designers educated in this legacy: what remains of the practitionership of designing when the industrial product disappears?

Contemplating the Social Designer's Practice

Designing for the common good says little about what designers design. One can say designers design policies, services, or organisations, but what kind, and policies and services for what? Designing services that incorporate execution by other people means that the designer is no longer the sole practitioner. Do designers still have a practice? Do designers become change agents; is their practice organising work, not specific to the content of the work? These questions deeply influence the identity of designers.

Perhaps designers lose their own practitionership the moment they start separating the thinking from the doing. Social designers create space for practitioners to execute their practice in a system that treats these practitioners as executors. Then designers are not in a position where they add direct value in the Lifeworld. Their value becomes indirect. Are designers then becoming what they are trying to change? Are they contributing to more layers of complexity, like middle management? At least social designers are using their 'practitionership' to assist others in making an impact in the Lifeworld. If that means sacrificing their own practice, it is a sacrifice designers should be willing to make.

And perhaps social designers' jobs should be temporary, to

help facilitate the change towards transformative governments and also a transformative way of working in other public organisations.
But at least designers are able to give it back to those who make the world go round.

Educating Social Designers

Social designers educated in the legacy of industrial product design clearly lack content knowledge and public domain knowledge. By this, I mean an understanding of politics and sociology, as well as knowledge of the domain they are going to work in. For example, lacking complete knowledge of medicine is not helpful when the value of designers lies in their ability to synthesise different factors. Industrial product designers have to know something about these factors, like engineering and marketing, to design a product. Designers also have to know something about medicine and the healthcare system to design policies and services for healthcare, at least if one follows the logic of designers.
Francis recalled her existential experience when she was designing something for fathers and daughters. It goes beyond language; designers feel it in their bodies. In the education of industrial product designers, there is room for these types of experiences. Designers can practise making moves, testing them, and reflecting on them—not only in theory but in practice, in the Lifeworld, with real people. The experience Francis recalled was relatively quickly achieved because a product can be tested relatively quickly.

For service design, this becomes more difficult to achieve within a short timeframe of education. Designers need not only people to test their product but also people to co-create a solution with and people to execute their tests. Not only knowledge of materials and construction is needed, but also knowledge of group dynamics and psychology of labour, for example. Then, if designers want to design public policies, that can take years to be fully implemented, and the value may be clear only after years. Yes, design students can design short-term interventions. But the experience of direct feedback on a product and what it can do in the Lifeworld is deeper and more personal.

The value of designers lies in their implicit practitionership, which they initially gained through designing industrial products, not in their use of forecasting methods. I wonder if future social designers who are actually educated as social designers may be less valuable than social designers who were not educated as social designers, simply because they missed the opportunity to experience what their designs do for/to people in the Lifeworld.

	Traditions in Public Administration	Leading principle in James' context	What is designed	Designed by
FOUNDATIONS	**Stability by Execution <1980**		**Practionership of Creation**	
	Constitutional (bureaucracy)	Follow procedures to execute the law	Everything artifical: created by humans	Designer
FOCUS	**Systemworld 1980-2000**		**Lifeworld**	
	Constitutional + Discretionary	Follow procedures + control execution of public services by the market	Product	Industrial product designer in close relation with experts
CONVERGENCE	**Collaboration 2000-2020**		**Co-Creation**	
	Constitutional + Discretionary + Collaborative	Follow procedures + control execution + we need to collaborate with parties	Service	Service designer in co-creation with the people that can make/break the service
DYNAMIC QUO	**Integration >2020 - Social Designers**			
	Constitutional + Discretionary + Collaborative + Transformative?	Follow procedures + control execution + collaborate + give direction in societal transitions		Social designer + key stakeholders from all parties + those with procedural say

Overview Inherited Baggage

Leading principle in Francis' practice	Designed in the Context of (viability)	Designed for (desirability)	Design realised by (feasibility)
Change by creation by allround practionership (thinking + doing)	Depends on what is designed	Depends on what is designed	Depends on what is designed
New products fulfil needs and bring value to consumers in the Lifeworld	A business	Consumers	Machines (production)
Creating together to ensure that people can bring value to consumers	A business	Consumers	Employees perhaps with people from other parties and users (execution)
Creating positive societal change through creation	Public administration (or public organisation)	Citizens and (or) for the politicians in order to execute legislations	Civil servants and employees from other parties (execution)

Say It With a Song

How Francis and James can dance together

‘Music is the universal language of mankind.’

Henry Wadsworth Longfellow

12.

'Knowing Me, Knowing You'

There are those that confuse being 'professional' with being serious. An improvisation guru once said: 'Take serious things playfully and take playful things seriously.' Because I am super serious about designers in public organisations, we should dance about it. Remember: Life is a song.

12.1 'Express Yourself'

Time for Madonna. Francis, next time someone asks you what you are good at, here are nine ways to Express Yourself.

1. Making Decisions and Getting Things Moving

I'm good at making decisions and acting on them, especially when a team or organisation gets stuck in the need for clear answers. I get us out of the 'We Need More Information Cycle.' When it's not my role to decide or when it's unclear who should, I bring the right people into the room so a decision can be made together.

2. Taking Action and Minimise Risk

As a designer, I make decisions even when outcomes aren't guaranteed. I combine thinking with doing — testing ideas in reality to learn what works. Acting isn't reckless; it's how I reduce risk. There's no perfect knowledge before action, so I treat each step as a way to check assumptions and move forward with purpose. I bring clarity through doing, not just planning and researching.

3. Showing How Things Are Connected

I'm good at explaining how actions, people, and results are connected. I create overviews or simple schemes to show how a policy or idea might work out, including its possible effects. I check the assumptions behind these ideas and often use drawings or objects to show how things are linked: like 'if I pull here, this will move there.'

4. Linking Values, Criteria, and Solutions

I'm able to shift between different levels: what we value, what that means for the solution, what the solution could be, and how it would work in real life. This helps make sure ideas don't just sound good, but actually make sense in practice.

5. Spotting Assumptions and Creating Openings

I'm good at noticing assumptions that shape how people think or act. By making these visible, I help create space for new ideas and different ways to step in or make change happen. I don't see situations as fixed or unchangeable: it is what it is. I see opportunities for change and to make a positive societal impact.

6. Taking the Politics Out of the Room

I use materials (like sketches, maps, or models) that include different viewpoints. This separates the stake from the stakeholder. It helps people talk about ideas without it becoming personal. When something is on the table, it's easier to discuss, even if you don't agree with it, because it's not tied to a person.

7. Helping People Hold Off on Judgment

Western education trains people to be critical. We are programmed to look for what's not working and what is not good about an idea. I flip that. I postpone judgment and first look at what is good or interesting about an idea. This opens up space for creativity and exploration. I can also increase this ability in other people.

8. Organising Meetings That Make Ideas Tangible

I design meetings that go beyond just talking. I use embodied thinking (doing, drawing, building) to help make complex ideas more concrete. This helps everyone in the room better understand what's going on and where they could act.

9. Understanding What's Holding People Back

I try to figure out why things are the way they are, what people need, and what is stopping them from moving forward. Not to coach them individually, but to see what is getting in the way of working together or making change happen.

12.2 'People are Strange, When You're a Stranger'

Again for Francis, this time a classic from The Doors. Here are five ways to empathise with James and his perspective. That is also real.

1. Respect the Intention of Procedures

That means practicing patience. From the legacy of industrial product, social designer value 'the new', it is a rush of dopamine. However, procedures things will take time and not all societal problems can be fixed.

2. Respect Knowledge and Learn the Logic

You don't know what they know. James is knowledgeable about his domain and about the way the organisational system functions. Respect that, and learn that logic. Not the logic of engineering nor art, not the logic of business, but the logic of public organisation, the logic of the system in which your public organisation is a part, the logic of politics. Either get formal education or learn it on the job (the hard way).

3. Respect their Brave Space

Understand that the 'not knowing part' is not exciting in civil service; it is terribly scary. Bravery in its slightest form should be supported. Take small steps. What is normal for you may be terrifying for your colleague. Empathise not only with citizens but also with your colleagues.

4. Your Design is not the End, Execution is

Whether you focus on desirability, viability, or feasibility, the biggest hurdle is not designing a new policy or service; it is making it a new reality, ensuring that the new design is actually executed. In an ideal world, designing a new service phase out the old service, and change flows naturally, so implementation is not needed. Yes, that would be nice.

5. Follow the money

Who pays decides. The person that is paying for you has the problem. The stake of this person determines the starting point and the desired outcome, at least at the start. Additionally, figuring out how budgets are distributed will give insight into power dynamics and how organisations are structured.

12.3 'Lift Me Up'

Francis may want to work in specific way but the 'job architecture' of a public administration or organisation cannot be ignored. To help Francis in her job as Service, Policy or Organisational designer, James could create conditions that help get the best out of Francis. So, for James we have a Lift me Up, from either David Guetta, Rihanna, Backstreet Boys, Five Fingers Death Punch, or Moby, your choice.

1. Define Value Created, not Problem Solved

Designers thrive on navigating tension—balancing lightness with strength or reconciling safety with freedom. Their work begins with a design brief that frames the paradox to overcome. Unlike project leaders who focus on fixed goals and data to track progress, designers engage in reflection-in-action, adapting as they go.

To create space for meaningful design, project plans should focus on added value rather than predefined solutions.

A business case framed in terms of value creation allows flexibility, making it easier to adjust as insights emerge during the process.

2. Involve Them Before You Start

Make space in the procedures for trusting them to run a process their way. Get approval for the procedure of not following the procedure. It is a paradox that we think there is a procedure for change. That also means finding a budget. If you want a good brief to secure more budget, get them on board earlier; they will ask questions you did not consider before.

3. Flip the Question

When goals are formulated as 'not this', it does not help in moving in a specific direction. For example, a government needs to protect itself from cybercriminality. 'We don't want to get hacked' is a different formulation than 'We want to be cybersecure.' Moving away from a situation does not provide any direction on where to go. If you have a personnel shortage, then the goal is to have enough staff. Even that is only a means to a purpose, which refers to the previous point: defining a project at the highest level of abstraction but in such a way that it moves toward something instead of away from a situation (see figure 40).

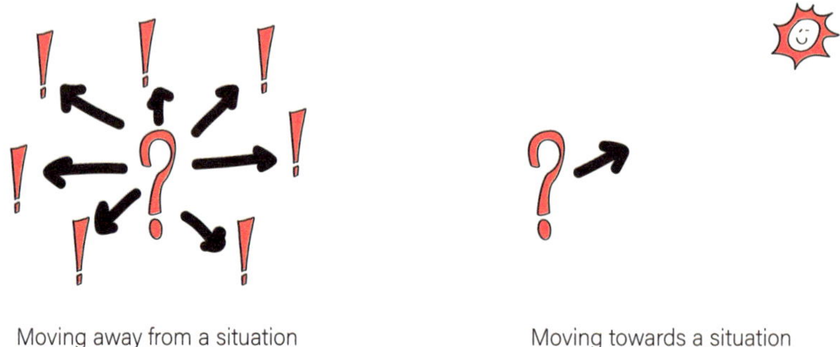

Figure 40: Moving away from, or moving towards a situation.

4. Include Stakeholders, Beginning to End

One of the hardest parts of design is getting the result accepted and implemented. Change only happens when those affected by the design are part of shaping it. Don't decide for stakeholders. Create space to decide with them. Designers need the stakeholders in the room to co-create, to talk with people, not about them. Inclusion builds ownership, and ownership drives execution.

5. They Aren't Judging You, They're Exploring

Designers often ask many questions, which isn't a criticism or an expectation that you have all the answers. Instead, designers are trying to understand the underlying system of a situation.

Questions like, 'Why is it done this way?' or 'Are we sure this is right?' are meant to explore, not to judge. This approach helps them clarify the practical situation and creates space to move forward collaboratively; they're aiming to make assumptions and associations explicit.

For those not accustomed to this questioning style, it can certainly feel overwhelming. If tdesigners don't understand why things are a certain way, they'll question it, especially if they don't see how a situation benefits the people it's meant to serve. But remember, the intention is to explore, not to judge.

6. Research Already Done? Let Them Do it Again

Designers' focus is not just on whether something works on paper, but on why it does or doesn't work in practice. The goal isn't to produce knowledge for its own sake, but to use it to create meaningful change. A formal report can be useful, but a conversation with just a few people may reveal insights no report contains. For designers, research is not a goal but a means to create value with intention. Therefore they may feel the need to do research themselves, their way.

2. Give Mental Support

The real mistake for a designer isn't trying something that fails, but persisting with it simply because it was part of the plan. This plan may stem from higher up, leaving designers to implement it rather than question it.
When the decision was political, politicians may promise the parliament solutions that the designer thinks: 'that solution does not solve the problem; it will create more problems!' Designers will recognise these situations quickly and feel frustrated by them. They will need mental support when that happens.

7. Pinpoint Success to Them

In the end, social designers have the intention to make an impact in the world. Sometimes, a great project that is ready to become the new procedure is canceled at the last minute due to political decisions. Frustrating, but part of the deal. Designers are used to fast results: project done, move on to the next. They may need some help in seeing the value of what they do, because for them it is not going fast enough. Help them celebrate the successes they cannot see as a success.

12.4 'You've Got the Love'

In my exploration of practitionership and ways of organising, I've emphasised the Head and the Hands: thinking and doing. But what is truly defining the work of social designers is the Heart. I genuinely believe social designers (and the people they work with) want to create a positive societal impact. That drive, that deep care, is the Heart at work.

The Heart appears at every level of what social designers do. When we communicate ideas, we don't just think about how to make something understandable (Head) or usable (Hands); we also want people to fall in love with it (Heart). The same goes for design processes: we strive to desire something in our Heart, imagine it in our Head, and bring it to life with our Hands.

'Ain't Nothing Gonna Break My Stride'

There's a beautiful paradox in how designers treat the Heart. They are objective about it—not just about their own, but others' too. What's real for someone emotionally may not be factually true, but it is true in their Heart. That matters. People make decisions by gut feeling. We can dismiss that, or we can embrace it. Social designers choose the latter. Where rationality might ignore the Heart, a social designer does not want to and can't afford to. We all cannot afford to. Especially not in times like these when some radical social events have happened on the world stage: a pandemic, a revival of the Cold War, the centuries-old Christian-Muslim conflict fought out in the Middle East, getting closer to Western civilisation, and democratic fractures in nations once seen as global leaders, shaking up power positions on the world stage. Not to mention the digital revolution that is happening because artificial intelligence technologies are becoming more advanced and accessible for people in their daily lives. Since the Enlightenment, we have devalued handwork in favor of headwork, in awe of machines. Now, AI may take over part of our headwork too. But even then, we will still have our Hearts. Designing is an act of creation. People like James and Francis need each other to create, to be resourcefulness, for resilience, for world peace, and a good hair day. Let's start today.

Epilogue

Francis has a new job interview for the position of Innovation Manager to help a Ministry with their Digital Transformation processes (in other words, Organisational Designer).
She is determined to go through the interview without using typical 'design terminology' as she did when she was being interviewed by Roy. Now she's being interviewed by Sam.

> 'Francis, what are your strengths?' asks Sam.
> 'I have a Bachelor's and Master's degree focused on working with uncertainty and creating change toward a desired situation. When we're innovating, we're dealing with the unknown. That requires a different kind of reasoning and decision-making than in stable situations. The world we work and live in is unpredictable, so we need to be able to adapt and deal with change. I'm comfortable making decisions when the outcomes are unclear. If it's not my role to decide, I highlight that there's no perfect certainty and that even not choosing is a choice. I also act decisively once decisions are made. I manage risk by taking small, careful steps, though I recognise that at some point, bigger decisions are needed to embed change in daily operations. I'm skilled at bringing together a broad range of stakeholders—not just the usual ones—and getting them to work collaboratively, rather than simply talk. I'm also good at identifying the

deeper needs of stakeholders. If I'm working in Digital Transformation, I wouldn't redesign people's jobs for them, especially when they know more about the subject than I do. My role is to support them in shaping their own work and to get people moving with me.' Francis stops talking, feeling satisfied with her answer.

'Okay. That is quite an answer', smiles Sam.

'What skills would you like to improve if you worked here?' she asks as her next question.

'I have a knowledge gap when it comes to the specific culture, norms, and history of this organisation. I don't yet understand where any resistance to change comes from or how much time day-to-day work for the Minister consumes. I'll also need to build trust, and I don't know yet how (mis)trustful people here might be. Some might have gone through multiple reorganisations that left a bitter taste in their mouths', answers Francis.

'Are you about organisational change?' asks Sam.

'Yes and no. The difference is that traditional organisational change often responds to structures like Taylorism, while my approach comes from a tradition of creation. Mine is more about doing and experiencing rather than talking or writing plans that get imposed from the top, to say it blunty. I know there are psychological aspects of change that experts understand better than I do. But by working with an open-minded change agent, I think we could learn a lot from each other.'

‘What would be the first thing you do when you start working here?’ continues Sam.
‘I’d begin by listening—having conversations to understand the unwritten rules, culture, and informal leadership of the organisation. I’d map these insights out visually as we talk’, answers Francis confidently.
‘Next, I’d bring together the people who influence both the problem and the solution. I’d help them understand each other’s mental models, compare views, and build a shared understanding of both the current and desired situations. Then we’d take small steps toward that goal, reflecting together after each one to see what’s working.’

-

‘Hey, how was that job interview you did a few weeks ago?’ James asks Francis.
‘Nailed it!’ Francis smiles.
‘Congratulations!’ James gives her a big hug.
‘Yeah, I knew exactly what to say. You remember that cousin of mine, Peter, who made me feel so small at my uncle’s birthday?’
James nods.
‘I met him last week’, Francis tells what happened.

‘Hey Francis, how are you? Still looking for a job?’ Peter asks cheerfully.
‘I’m fine, thanks. Actually, I have a job now, how kind of

you to ask', Francis replies, a touch sarcastically.
'Oh yes? And what is it you are again?' Peter says.
'A social designer', Francis says proudly.
'Right, a social designer... remind me what that is?' Peter smirks, making air quotes.
'I help organisations adapt to change', Francis begins. 'Society's complex, and change happens fast. I help people move from endless talking to creating small, meaningful steps toward better situations. I organise workshops, get stakeholders working together, and help them see new perspectives, not just in their heads, but in ways they can really feel.'
'Feel it in their bodies, eh? I feel other things in my body. Get it?' Peter laughs.
Francis thinks, 'pig', but just smiles.
'It's easy to sit behind a spreadsheet, but hearing people's real stories changes how you see things and inspires solutions you wouldn't have thought of otherwise. Small changes can make a big difference. If you like, I can help you step away from your computer, for a fee of course.'

'Ha! You really put him in his place', James grins.
'I wanted to, yes', Francis admits. 'And it felt good for a moment. But actually, that's what designing is about too, isn't it? Seeing different realities and bringing them together. His reality is true for him, and I have to work with that if I want to create real change.'
'That's exactly why you're good at what you do', James

says.

Francis smiles. ‘Thanks. I’m glad I kept my cool. In the end, I think I even got through to him a little.’

Designing a Book (sort of)

Is writing a book like designing a book? Being a designer myself, I feel obliged to answer this reflective question: what did I learn from this writing and/or design process?

I started this book in late 2023, after several promotion thesis proposals that left my supervisors confused and me frustrated. ‘What is the frustration you are actually trying to dig into?’ they’d ask. Well, I had one frustration: not being able to articulate that. For academic research, I had to be able to answer these questions, and I couldn’t. So I stopped stumbling through explaining and started writing a book instead: this is what I want to say.

In a year and a half, I may have written the equivalent of three books. I could’ve stuck with a focus on creativity in the public domain, in all its richness, my main expertise. But no, I had to wrestle with what I couldn’t yet articulate in informal conversations. I felt there was something more urgent to say; the creativity story I could always do later as my second book. So for this book, I sort of had the idea of the value that I wanted to bring, but the story remained foggy in my brain. Did I have a plan? Not so much. Like with designing, you just need to start. I have gone through all the emotional ups and downs that are part of creating. I did a classic version of 'thinking by doing'.

What is ironic is that I always tell my students not to write their reports the way I write: 'Start with a clear structure, your narrative, then start writing'. I'm not telling them that anymore. What writing is for designing a story, drawing is for designing products. I remember a Chicago professor once talking about two types of writing: horizontal writing, which is writing to think, and vertical writing, which is writing to communicate. It is basically the two ways designers use visuals to think and to communicate. What I will advise students is to choose between vertical and horizontal writing, if they are able to. I wrote diagonally; I'm not sure I would recommend that.

I had many insights while writing this book. Two major ones. First, the key realisation while writing: when you design services, you are organising work; you're shaping how others do it. That blew my mind.
Second, the practitionership of designers—losing the practitionership without the product and perhaps creating space for others to actually execute their practice (instead of what is said)—is a key paradox in my book. The second one is the idea that the more theoretically we educate social designers, the less valuable they might become, which is a paradox I have to deal with as an educator of social designers.

I did something else that was important to me: I finally managed to connect the Rhinish-way of organising and designing. The two concepts had been orbiting each other in my brain since 2011, the first time I got in contact with the Rhinish-way of organising. Now they've met, even though it is just a sidenote in the book, for me, it was an important ingredient to integrate into the story.

Know that I changed the title of my book six times. I also had:

- The Roots of Social Design
- The Secret Stories of Social Design
- Understanding Social Design
- Designing in Civil Service
- The Happy Social Designer

And countless AI-generated subtitles. Thanks, AI (but also no thanks).

Looking back, it took me over fifteen years to order my thoughts in such a way that I could write them down for others to read. I still want to change things. But that's design for you. Just as throwing your work into the world, knowing there is always someone who will trash it anyway, is part of designing. Still, sharing your ideas, imperfect as they are, is better than never putting them out at all. I'm immensely proud that I brought this project to an end. Now, I have at least fifteen years of people to thank.

Thanks to...

Thanks to BIS Publishers, especially Harm, for recognising value in my thoughts and taking the leap of trust to publish my work. To Pieter Knippenberg, who edited my texts and many more that didn't make it to this final version, thanks for your patience and great rewrites.
To Kristal, Myron, Senna, and Patrick for taking the time and effort to read unfinished versions and give feedback, which was tremendously valuable and daunting at the same time.
Thanks to all the people who shared their stories and wisdom with me throughout the years. Especially to all the people who embrace this Rhinish concept: you share my values, and I believe you are making the world more beautiful. Also, thanks to the civil servants, students, and colleagues—past and present—whom I unknowingly used to test my ideas in conversation, and from whom I got great dialogue in return.
Frido and Mathieu, thank you for making the effort to help me pursue a promotion, and also for letting me fail (so far) at that—pushing me to pivot in a direction that led me to write this book.
Some colleagues deserve extra attention. Thanks to Annemiek for critically cheering me on, especially in the beginning of my writing process. To the team of Minor Connected Creativity for being my home base at work—especially Barbera and Katrina. Barbera, who has the natural gift of making people feel good about themselves, supporting me in exactly the way I needed, when I needed it. And Katrina, for being the person I can turn

to for deep conversations about creativity and for sharing student jokes—a great sense of humor. I love the way our threesome can read and write together.

In my personal life, I don't tend to talk much about my thoughts on designing or creativity. I feel easily misunderstood, miss the words to explain myself, and feel reluctant to talk for hours about my ideas. From now on, I can say: read my book :).
Thanks to my family and friends, simply for being there and taking my mind off business—you know who you are. Thanks to Bas, my husband, whom I kept quite in the dark about the content of this book, but who tried to support me in every way he could, creating time for me to write.
To my parents, who also have no clue what I'm writing about, but who taught me self-belief and the idea that I'm a capable person. That idea helped when imposter-syndrome sneaked up on me during the process.
To my kids, to whom I explained that I was writing a book. They thought that was awesome and left me to it when deadlines were approaching—though they did complain about my absence from the living room in the months before the deadline. Their support means the world to me. I hope I can be an example of following your heart while using your head and hands.

References

Albert, M. (1997). Capitalism against capitalism (P. Haviland, Trans.). Whurr. (Original work published 1991).

Archer, B. (1968). The structure of design processes. Royal College of Art.

Baer, J. (2015). The Importance of Domain-Specific Expertise in Creativity. Roeper Review, 37(3), 165–178.

Braams, R. B., Wesseling, J. H., Meijer, A. J., & Hekkert, M. P. (2021). Legitimizing transformative government: Aligning essential government tasks from transition literature with normative arguments about legitimacy from Public Administration traditions. Environmental Innovation and Societal Transitions, 39, 191–205.

Brouwer, J. J., & Moerman, P. (2005). Angelsaksen versus Rijnlanders. Garant.

Buchanan, R. (1992). Wicked problems in design thinking. Design Issues, 8(2), 5–21.

Clarke, A., & Craft, J. (2019). The twin faces of public sector design: Policy design and design thinking. Governance, 32(1), 5–21.

Compton, M. E., & 't Hart, P. (2019). How to 'see' great policy successes: A field guide to spotting policy successes in the wild. In M. E. Compton & P. 't Hart (Eds.), Great policy successes (pp. 1–30). Oxford University Press.

Conference on Design Methods. (1963). In J. C. Jones & D. G. Thornley (Eds.), Conference on design methods: Papers presented at the Conference on Systematic and Intuitive Methods in Engineering, Industrial Design, Architecture and Communications, London, September 1962 (222 pp.). Pergamon Press.

Cross, N. (2006). Designerly ways of knowing. Springer.

Cross, N. (2007). Forty years of design research. Design Studies, 28(1), 1–4.

Dorst, K. (2011). The core of 'design thinking' and its application. Design Studies, 32, 521-532.

Hermus, M., van Buuren, A., & Bekkers, V. (2020). Applying design in public administration: A literature review to explore the state of the art. Policy & Politics, 48(1), 21–48.

Jiang, H., & Gero, J. S. (2014). Comparing engineering and industrial design students: The effects of different design education on the design cognition. Design Studies, 35(6), 559–576.

Johansson-Sköldberg, U., Woodilla, J., & Çetinkaya, M. (2013). Design thinking: Past, present and possible futures. Creativity and Innovation Management, 22(2), 121–146.

Kimbell, L. (2011). Rethinking design thinking: Part 1. Design and Culture, 3(3), 285–306.

Lewis, J. M., McGann, M., & Blomkamp, E. (2020). When design meets power: Design thinking, public sector innovation and the politics of policymaking. Policy & Politics, 48(1), 111–130.

Lloyd, P. (2017). From design methods to future-focused thinking: 50 years of design research. Design Studies, 48, A1–A8.

Meyer, R. E., & Boxenbaum, E. (2010). Exploring European-ness in organization research. Organization Studies, 31(6), 737–755.

Osborne, S. P., & Brown, L. (2011). Innovation, public policy and public services delivery in the UK: The word that would be king? Public Administration, 89(4), 1335–1350.

Peters, B. G. (1994). Managing the hollow state. International Journal of Public Administration, 17(3–4), 739–756.
Rittel, H. W. J., & Webber, M. M. (1973). Dilemmas in a general theory of planning. Policy Sciences, 4(2), 155–169.
Roozenburg, N. F. M., and Eekels, J. (1995). Productontwerpen, structuur en methoden (2nd print). Lemma BV.
Rothstein, B. (2012). Political legitimacy for public administration. In B. G. Peters & J. Pierre (Eds.), The SAGE handbook of public administration (pp. 357–369). SAGE.
Schön, D. A. (1987). The reflective practitioner: How professionals think in action. Basic Books. (Original work published 1983).
Schön, D. A. (1992). Designing as reflective conversation with the materials of a design situation. Research in Engineering Design, 3(3), 131–147.
Simon, H. A. (1969). The sciences of the artificial. MIT Press.
Stappers, P. J., Sleeswijk Visser, F., & van Boeijen, A. (2023). Design labels: The words that divide & unite us. In 15th International Conference of the European Academy of Design (Blucher Design Proceedings, 11(4)). Blucher.
Stout, M. (2017). Logics of legitimacy: Three traditions of public administration praxis. Taylor & Francis.
Torfing, J., & Triantafillou, P. (2016). Enhancing public innovation by transforming public governance. Cambridge University Press.
Tromp, N., & Vial, S. (2022). Five components of social design: A unified framework to support impact, reflection and dialogue. *The Design Journal*, 25(1), 1–21.
Van Arkel, T., and Tromp, N. (2024) What Do Designers Bring To The Table? Identifying Key Design Competencies When Designing For Societal Challenges In The Public Sector, in Gray, C., Ciliotta Chehade, E., Hekkert, P., Forlano, L., Ciuccarelli, P., Lloyd, P. (eds.), DRS2024: Boston, 23–28 June, Boston, USA.
Van Buuren, A., Lewis, J. M., Peters, B. G., & Voorberg, W. (2020). Improving public policy and administration: Exploring the potential of design. Policy & Politics, 48(1), 13–19.
Van Soest, P. (2021, November 17). Leerlingen de dupe van 'flauwekul'-lessen op school: 'Methodes deugen niet.' Algemeen Dagblad.
Visser, W. (2010). Schön: Design as a reflective practice. Collection, Parsons Paris School of Art and Design, Art + Design & Psychology, 2, 21–25.
Wilson, J. Q. (1989). Bureaucracy: What government agencies do and why they do it. Basic Books.

Index

E

F

L

M

N

O

P

R

S

T

U

V

W